NEW YORK

POP CITY
—Guide—

NEW YORK

David Brun-Lambert
Aurélie Pollet
Michael Prigent
David Tanguy

CHÊNE

Contents

= Map pages 6–7

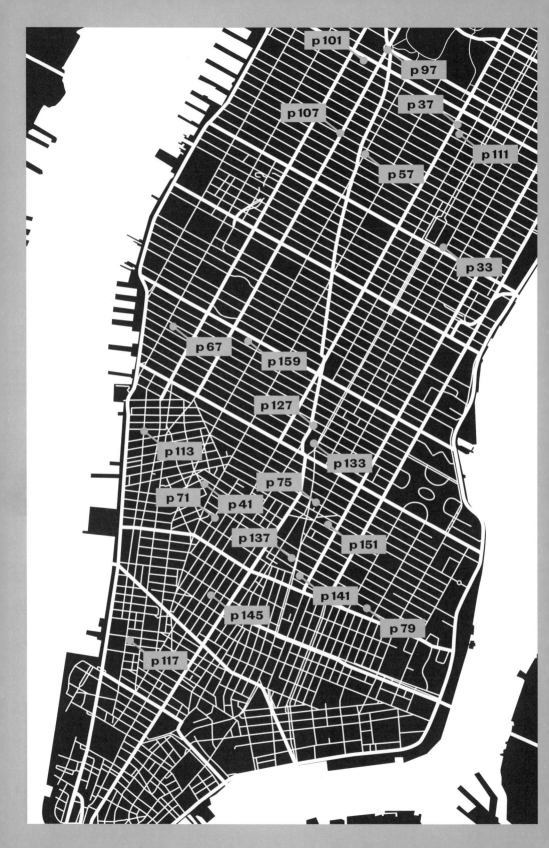

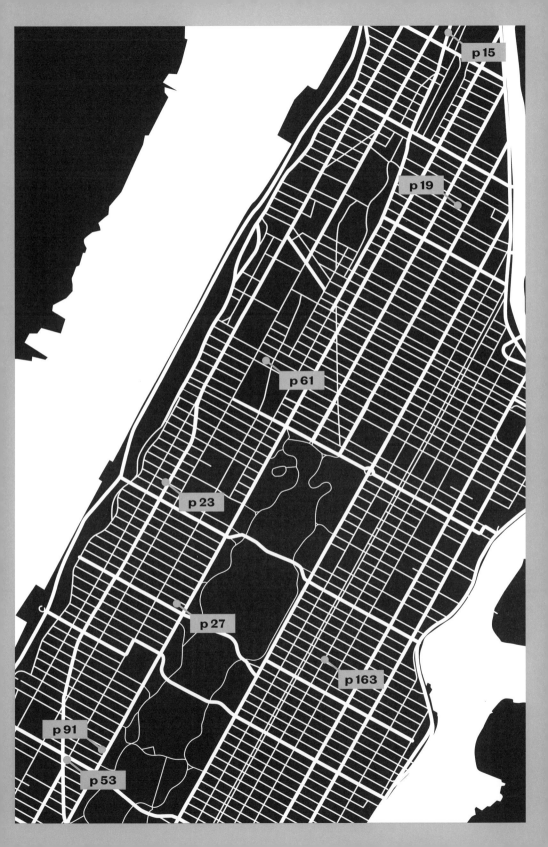

p 15

p 19

p 61

p 23

p 27

p 163

p 91

p 53

Introduction

Everyone knows New York. Everyone loves the Big Apple, often without having set foot in this iconic city. Over the past century and right up to the present, hundreds of songs, films, books, TV series and artistic figures have celebrated its DNA, painting a detailed picture of this city that is at once complex, contrasting, exciting and poisonous. Fascinating. *All the time.*

Lower East Side, from the paved side streets of SoHo to the comforts of Greenwich Village, the mysteries of Chinatown to the venom of the Bowery, from the splendour of the Upper East Side to the industrial scenes of TriBeCa or Chelsea, New York is a city-world of conflicts: one in a constant state of flux, where in order to *exist* you must, first and foremost, *fight*. A place in which no-one and nowhere is ever quite what they seem.

At once joyful and deceitful, seductive and violent, captivating and disconcerting, the Big Apple has established itself as a powerful driving force for creation and modernity throughout the twentieth century. It is a land of asylum for communities who, together, have formed the American cultural identity. Since the 1910s, music, literature, film and art have depicted New York and what it means to live in a post-industrial age at the heart of a multicultural Babylon.

Having become a symbol of the economic power of the United States, 'Gotham City' has kept its finger on the pulse in a way that no other place could. The city that never sleeps is fast, loud, cruel and sexualised. It has successively reinvented itself as a world capital for jazz and folk, the birthplace of punk rock and hip hop, a mecca for Beat literature, for clubbing, art and indie cinema. With its artistic performances, sculptures, architecture and photography (often forgotten), NYC is a crossroads that welcomes all forms of expression.

These artistic movements and currents have also led to the invention of innovative new spaces for creation within the city: warehouses, lofts, disused brownfield sites, etc.

Going for a walk in present-day New York means retracing the history of the events that have formed the basis of a large part of today's common cultural heritage. These are the countless bars and clubs, the dozens of studios and theatres, the basements and workshops where the artists who are cult icons today lived and created, loved and despaired, meditated or blazed through their lives.

The majority of the places where these creative processes happened have now disappeared, being replaced over the decades by commercial areas or private apartments. However, for those who know where to look, New York, from Harlem to Brooklyn, still provides us with a ghost map of the routes our pop heroes used to take.

This book looks at Billie Holiday, Jack Kerouac, Andy Warhol and Robert De Niro in *Taxi Driver* : four key artistic figures whose lives are inextricably linked to the cultural history of the Big Apple. Whether you decide to take to the streets or read from the comfort of your sitting room, this first volume from the *Pop City* collection allows you to put yourselves into these icons' shoes. During a fictional walk past real addresses, all of which are linked to their personal stories, the book allows you to walk in the shoes of each of these characters and discover what each of them saw, tasted, felt and experienced on any particular day.

David Brun-Lambert, Aurélie Pollet,
Michael Prigent, David Tanguy

Billie Holiday

'The first time I heard her voice, I thought it came from another world,' said Nina Simone about Billie Holiday, the iconic jazz singer who is counted among the most influential singers of the twentieth century.

Born in Philadelphia on 7 April 1915 as Eleanora Fagan, she had a troubled childhood in Baltimore. Shuttled between one household and another, experiencing prison, and then rape as a teenager, she ended up joining her mother, Sadie, in Harlem at the age of fourteen. There, she became immersed in the hectic lifestyle of 133rd Street, also known as Swing Street, and her singing career kicked off in the speakeasies there. After being heard by the producer John Hammond, Billie Holiday, as she came to be known within jazz circles, recorded her first record with the clarinettist Benny Goodman, performed at the Apollo Theater and started a successful collaboration with the saxophonist Lester Young.

'Lady Day' became a key figure of New York nights, mixing with high-class society and working with conductors like Duke Ellington, Artie Shaw and Count Basie. In 1939, at Café Society she unveiled 'Strange Fruit', the first American protest song.

Sinking into a dependence on alcohol and opiates and stuck in a chaotic love life, things went from bad to worse for Holiday and she ended up in prison in 1947. At the start of the 1950s, she relaunched her career and experienced some success, but her heart just wasn't in it. Billie, a tragic figure, recorded her final album, *Lady in Satin*, in 1955. Her death was announced four years later, on 17 July 1959. From Frank Sinatra to Esther Philips, from Dianne Reeves to Cassandra Wilson, her work has fascinated many generations of musicians.

7 a.m.

W 155th St

St Nicholas Ave

9 a.m.

W 145th St

W 135th St

Henry Hudson Pkwy

Broadway

Amsterdam Ave

St Nicholas Ave

Frederick Douglass Blvd

7th Ave

Lenox Ave

5th Ave

Park Ave

7 a.m.
Duke Ellington's
apartment
935 St Nicholas Avenue

9 a.m.
Florence
Williams's brothel
151 West 140th Street

10 a.m.
Mom Holiday's
9 West 99th Street

12 a.m.
Billie Holiday's
apartment
26 West 87th Street

20 April 1939

Duke Ellington's apartment

935 St Nicholas Avenue

7 a.m. One club leads to another. Cigarettes. Alcohol. Kisses given, taken, snatched. Laughter spurts out through the wisps of marijuana, while friends take out their instruments and start to play, erupting into noise. 'Hey Lady! Get moving!', they shout. Lost in the arms of a lover whose name she can't call to mind at that time of night, she laughs, a night-weary beauty queen, reigning over her world of currently dishevelled men. What had she been doing before ending up at Duke's alongside Highbridge Park and Harlem River? There had definitely been a detour via The Daisy Chain (Lenox Avenue & 141st Street), that at least she can remember: the 'meeting house' that Ellington himself had paid tribute to ('Swingin' at The Daisy Chain', 1937). What had happened next? An alcoholic breakfast at Amy Ruth's (113 West 116th Street) at the heart of Harlem, three blocks from Marcus Garvey Park, where the junkies hang around in the mornings. Then more cigarettes. More drinks. 'What's this moonshine?', she cries. 'Where's the cognac?' There's no way to find it among the empty bottles abandoned on the parquet floor of this stylish apartment.

She takes a look around her. It's a small miracle. Usually it's impossible to get all of the members of her clique together in the same place and in the same early hours, but this time they're all there. Jimmie Lunceford, Fletcher Henderson and Chick Webb. Benny Carter,

Ted Wilson, Coleman Hawkins and Jimmy Harrison.
There's even that pest Ethel Waters, the 'green bean' as
Billie calls her, who's always sucking up to Irving Mills,
Duke's manager. The maestro himself rules over his world
with the nonchalance that Lady admires. Is the admiration
reciprocated? She is uncertain. Four years earlier,
the producer John Hammond had convinced Ellington to
hire Billie for *Symphony in Black*, a nine-minute musical
written on the corner of a table. In fact it was the tale of a
stupid love triangle, in which Lady played the grief-stricken
wife, an appropriate role for her. Fred Waller had directed it,
the Paramount had shown it and the girl from Baltimore had
seen her career take off – just as Hammond said it would.
Another cigarette, and now Lady sees herself sitting on the
floor of the studio in Astoria, lamenting 'The Saddest
Tale': *Saddest tale on land or sea | Was when my man walked out
on me | My man's gone | I feel so alone...*
She was just nineteen years old. With a clear complexion
and full chest, she was built to say it all. With no effort at
all, her charm seemed to enchant everybody around her.
Four years later? Here she is in Duke's lounge, improvising
on a stride started by Henderson, while around her the
'motherfuckers', as she calls them, relay on piano or sax.
Others are knocking back drinks, drowning their sorrows
near the bar. How many glasses of gin has she drunk this
evening? And how many joints have been smoked since she
sang at Café Society ten hours earlier? Who knows.
As tiredness hasn't reared its head, she goes for an improv
around 'Moody Indigo' or 'Riffin' the Scotch' as Ellington
gently despatches his guests.

'I've been told that nobody sings the word "hunger" like I do. Or the word "love". Maybe I remember what those words are all about.'

Billie Holiday

Florence Williams' brothel

151 West 140ᵗʰ Street

9 a.m. From Duke's apartment, Holiday takes a cab straight down St Nicholas Avenue. She ignores Lester 'Prez' Young who is sleeping by her side, his mouth open and head tilted back. They follow Morningside Park and doze while Harlem's brownstones, those typical New York buildings, pass by on either side. Nowadays, there is nothing left of the calm, leafy neighbourhood that previously housed Jewish, Irish and German families. Since the 1920s, the black people who moved up from the south in search of work have changed it completely. North of 110th St, instead of the farms and residential areas that you could still see thirty years earlier, there are only abandoned and deteriorated buildings, overcrowded slums that the authorities have always taken good care to ignore. Because of this, these nine square kilometres where 200,000 people survive on wheeling and dealing, is still a safe place to go to at night without risking your neck, and have fun until sunrise without spending a cent. A short time ago, Harlem and 133rd street had a set of clubs, speakeasies, brothels, dance clubs, smoke houses and gambling dens that were unique in America. While prohibition was in full force elsewhere, here they managed to adapt. And while segregation was ruling America? In this destitute area, neglected by street cleaners and social services alike, they worked with it. The rich white folk came here each evening to have fun, and on Swing Street a host of clubs opened up. There was Tillie's, The Nest, The Mad House, The Yeah Man and The Bright Spot. And also Chicken Stack, Elmira, Bank's, Harry Hansberry's Clam House, and so on.

Billie had discovered this derelict, harsh and exciting environment at the age of fourteen. She had just left Baltimore. At that time, she was still known as Eleanora Fagan, the abandoned daughter of Sadie Fagan and Clarence Holiday, an absent father and virtuoso guitarist who would later play in Fletcher Henderson's orchestra. When she was asked where she was from, the young girl would answer in that surly, hurried tone that she curiously never lost: her mother had become pregnant at nineteen and her father refused to assume responsibility for the child. Sadie was rejected by her family and slaved at Philadelphia hospital to pay for the straw mattress where Eleanora was finally born. Then, the return to Baltimore. The little girl was put in a foster home. Later on she ran away from a catholic school, preferring to work a series of jobs and make her own money. Clarence visited her from time to time, but never for very long. He made fun of her fondness for getting into scraps and called her 'Bill' for a laugh. Very soon, she discovered Baltimore's nightlife. At that time it was a city of pleasures. Then there was her mother's failed marriage to a certain Mr Gough and, after that, Sadie's mysterious trips to New York every weekend. There were the neighbours who talked, gossiped and found fault. And very soon the comments: 'whore', 'tart'. Eleanora hung around with the kids from the block, sang obscene blues and snuck into the cinema to admire Billie Dove, her idol, in B-movies. Anyone who keeps on shoplifting eventually gets caught and she ended up in a reform school. On leaving the school, there was the rape. She was just eleven years old. She was tall for her age and well developed as well. Then, the arrival in New York, and adolescence. Sadie took her to a Harlem boarding house where, she said, a prepaid room was waiting for her...

From the back seat of the cab, Lady now contemplates this ordinary-looking building, jammed between today's Malcolm X and Adam Clayton Powell Jr boulevards, and reads the words above the porch: Pinkney Court. She says them out loud, as if to savour them. 'Pinkney Court.'

Until recently, this address was a famous brothel run
by Florence Williams, one of the best-known madams of
140th Street.
It was this very same Madam Williams for whom Sadie
worked, and who turned Eleanora into a call girl at twenty
dollars a go. 'Prez' wakes up abruptly. 'Where are we?'
And the boss orders the chauffeur, 'Get going!'

Mom Holiday's

9 West 99th Street

10 a.m. Here is Sadie, 'the Duchess', Billie's anxious mother, hurrying towards her daughter. To the west is Riverside Drive, and one block east is Broadway. It's a pretty neighbourhood. New Yorkers call it Manhattan Valley. A few months previously, Billie and her mother still lived here together, above the grill house where Mom Holiday served typical southern dishes: pig's trotters, kidney beans, rice, fried onions. 'I wanted Mom kept busy to stop her worrying and watching over me', said Lady, to justify the money she had invested in the restaurant. Intrusive, consumed with guilt, worried that one day her daughter would abandon her, Sadie was like a vampire; the previously mild woman had become a shrew. Quarrels formed part of their DNA and tensions were commonplace between her and Eleanora (as she insisted on calling her daughter). There was so much to be forgotten. And nothing could be repaired. Of course, it was hard to forget the events that had peppered Lady's childhood, which included the raid that she had been a victim of at fifteen, and in which 'the Duchess' had abandoned her again.

The Great Depression was in full force. The authorities had suddenly become alarmed by the awful hygiene conditions in which Harlem's inhabitants were living: a million and a half people completely dependent on social aid. And the administration's response? To swoop in and make multiple arrests. This is how, at the age of fifteen, Eleanora appeared before judge Jean Norris, the first women magistrate in New York, on a charge of 'soliciting'. 'Those were rotten days', wrote Billie in her autobiography *Lady Sings the Blues* (1956).

'Women [...] who worked as maids, cleaned office buildings, were picked up on the street on their way home from work and charged with prostitution. If they could pay, they got off. If they couldn't they went to court, where it was the word of some dirty grafting cop against theirs.[1]'
The result for the young girl was a sentence of 100 days in Women's House of Detention, a sordid reformatory on Welfare Island (nowadays Roosevelt Island). Then a forced period at Welfare Island Hospital. Eleanora arrived there in perfect health. She didn't undergo a medical examination. However, they operated on her. For what? Today, as Sadie sits opposite her in the already heaving restaurant asking questions about Eleanor Roosevelt, who had been at one of her concerts the other night, Holiday still keeps quiet about the operation she suffered. However, it's a secret she confided to a lover a few weeks previously: 'My ovaries are shot, you know...'

1 *Lady Sings the Blues*, Billie Holiday and William Dufty, Broadway Books, 1956

'A kiss that is
never tasted,
is forever and
ever wasted.'

Billie Holiday

Billie Holiday's apartment

12 a.m. Bessie Smith's 'Crazy Blues' is playing on the gramophone. Then Louis Armstrong's 'West End Blues'. Another drink downed, the lounge windows wide open, 'Prez' lying asleep on the sofa. He's a deep sleeper, this guy. Lady grants herself a bath, cigarette between her lips, while the smell of spring slowly spreads through apartment 1B. It's a lovely day in Manhattan, and even here you can smell the fragrance of the cedars from nearby Central Park. Lady will go there again in a few hours, as soon as she feels like herself again. Just like the previous day, she'll be seen following 87th Street to Central Park West, turning south to join 85th Street Traverse and finally joining the Bridle Path, with its squirrels, swans and ducks that gather around the reservoir. It's a ritual walk that she has taken ever since she moved to this pretty neighbourhood. The last time, leaving a night at the Savoy Ballroom (596 Lenox Avenue), in the early hours of the morning, she had joined the park at 106th Street to wander around Great Hill. on her own. It was a Saturday. There were families already setting up their lunches. Children ran in all directions, yelling and sweaty, the first spring rays shining on their sleepy faces. Billie had looked at this family and thought of the horde of children she would never have.

Right now, her family is 'Prez' who she can hear snoring in her Regency style bed. It's Kenneth Hollon, with whom she took her first steps on Jamaica Avenue in the old days, making $100 in tips in one night. A fortune that was then spent on gin, dope and royal tips. It's Bobby Henderson, with whom she'd brought down the house one free-wheeling night at Brownie's (154 West 133rd Street),

'You can be up to
your boobies in
white satin,
with gardenias
in your hair and
no sugar cane for
miles, but you can
still be working
on a plantation.'

Billie Holiday

an underground club on Jungle Alley. Billie was already singing 'All of Me' and 'Georgia on My Mind' for frenzied audiences. A few months later, she would play the same repertoire to the wealthy customers at Pod's & Jerry's (133rd Street & 7th Avenue). At first she had hated this venue. The singers had to bend over the tables to collect the folded notes that had been left. Lady refused to do so, but very soon the filthy-rich customers deigned to stand up and slip twenty dollar bills into her hand. The other girls hated her for this. They were just jealous! Copy cats, above all, reduced to imitating Ethel Waters. Billie sang as if she were wailing, or crying: improvising, taking her audience hostage and making a killing every show. Then she would blow the lot. She laughed. It was a happy time. The happiest she would ever know.

W 57th St

9th Ave

5th Ave

E 66th St

W 59th St

W 57th St

9th Ave

8th Ave

E 59th St

E 57th St

8 p.m.

5th Ave

E 42nd St

5 p.m.

Broadway

Park Ave

2nd Ave

1st Ave

FDR Drive

E 34th St

5 p.m.
Commodore Hotel
109 East 42nd Street

8 p.m.
Columbia Records Studio
711 Fifth Avenue

10 p.m.
Café Society
1 Sheridan Square

Commodore Hotel

109 East 42nd Street

5 p.m. Dressed in a figure-hugging, black, pleated dress, adorned with a heavy pearl necklace, a wide-brimmed hat and green suede high heels, Billie makes her entrance into the bar of the Commodore, a hotel that was built in 1919 opposite Grand Central Terminal (89 East & 42nd Street). This is the heart of Midtown: business and dough. Just one year ago, she wouldn't have even been allowed in. Just imagine: while on tour with the conductor Artie Shaw, the management of the nearby Lincoln Hotel (between 44th & 45th Street on 8th Avenue) had even stopped her from entering the elevator and the bar, where the orchestra was waiting. Of course, the customers could have complained and the police might have been called. They couldn't risk the scandal, just for the sake of allowing a black woman to play that evening. Consequence: each time she came to sing, she had to enter and leave the building via the kitchens, without hanging around. And between two sets? She would pace around outside on 45th Street where there was nothing going on because everyone was seven blocks north around 'Swing Street': the 52nd, where you could hear the roaring sounds of Kelly's Stable (137 West 52nd Street), the Famous Door (West 52nd Street) and the Onyx (35th West 52nd Street), Billie performed in this last club soon after 'Summertime' (1936) was recorded.

Now things are different. Now, Lady Day is a star. Billie was the best paid singer on 52nd Street. Put her name at the top of a poster and it was a sure thing that the show would sell out. Because of this, she was now welcomed with respect at the Commodore bar. For this reason, the well-dressed white women turned with admiration as she passed, 'Did you see who that was?' And then there was Milt Gabler who starts inviting her over to his table, giving her all his respect.

Gabler ran the Commodore Music Shop (136 East 42nd Street), a shop selling renowned jazz records that had recently become a high-end label. He knew a thing or two about the music business, but for this young guy from Harlem, there was no question of extending his label without first signing Billie. Later on, after Lady, he would go on to produce Lionel Hampton, Ella Fitzgerald and Louis Armstrong. A drink. And then another. They talk about the riots that broke out in Harlem last year. The closure of the speakeasies, the roundup of prostitutes. The crash of the nightlife on 133rd Street, the promoters who reduced their programmes to the bare minimum and the musicians who paid the price – a destiny that Billie hadn't shared. However, from that moment onwards, a black anger could be detected in her blues. It was this anger that one day prompted Ralph Cooper, the star presenter at the Apollo Theater (253 West 125th Street), to say, 'You never heard the such singing. It ain't the blues – I don't know what it is.' A sadness with no remedy. And Billie has now found a song to express this sorrow for which no God exists. It's called 'Strange Fruit', a title that Milt Gabler just has to release. The proof: he pays $500 in advance and promises 1,000 more when the song is released in July. The recording is planned that very evening at Café Society (1 Sheridan Square), where Billie has had a three-month run, and where John Hammond, her 'discoverer', producer and 'benefactor', now refuses to visit her...

'No two people on earth are alike, and it's got to be that way in music, or it isn't music.'

Billie Holiday

Columbia
Records Studio

711 Fifth Avenue

8 p.m. She's late. That will definitely get on Hammond's nerves. But what can she do? First, she drank at her meeting with Gabler, but that's OK, she could handle it. At the age of ten, she was already elbow bending with small-time thugs in drinking competitions, knocking back bootleg liquor. When her meeting is over, she finds Sonny White, her 'sweetheart', waiting for her in front of the Commodore. This time, he'd done things right: a cab on 42nd Street with a full bag of dope and a bottle of gin stashed on the back seat. After that, they drove at random around the dodgy streets of the Theater District, and White helped her to forget herself. Oh, it'd been gossiped about for a long time: Billie's men, she allowed them to do anything they liked. And in return, they used her and gave nothing in return. In her immediate circle of friends, her turbulent love life had always been a subject of conversation. They were amazed that she inevitably sank into dependence and put up with such bad treatment: stolen money, blows dealt. And how could she really *love* guys like Ben Webster, Louis McKay, John Levy (called 'Al Capone'), Joe Guy and Jimmy Monroe? They were real brutes. From the gutter. Billie, whose body had already been soiled by the rape, inflicted punishment on herself. With Sonny White there was no difference. He also dominated her, but unlike the others, he'd asked for her hand in marriage. In May, the magazine *Melody Maker* would announce their wedding. The party would take place... but not the wedding ceremony.

She enters Columbia Records Studio, two steps away from 52nd Street. It's dead in there. Why would John Hammond insist on meeting her in this place? Perhaps it was because he was scared of causing a scandal.

This guy, a Yale graduate from a good New York family and one of the most influential figures in the American music business, had done a lot for her. First it had been an article in Melody Maker in which, after having heard her at Covan's, he'd written, 'This month, there has been a real find in the person of a singer called Billie Holiday [...] though only eighteen she weighs over 200 pounds, is incredibly beautiful and sings as well as anybody I ever heard.' A short time later, Benny Goodman came to one of the young lady's recordings, and after that she was booked at Alhambra (2116 Adam Clayton Powell Jr. Boulevard) and at Savoy Ballroom (596 Lenox Avenue) with the Count Basie Orchestra. Later still, with Hammond's guidance, she recorded 'You're Too Lovely to Last', 'Under a Blue Jungle Moon' and 'Everything Happens for the Best'. Then 'More Than You Know' and 'It's Easy to Blame the Weather'. All the classics. Titles that the first lady of swing had tried her hand at before coming unstuck: she understood that the other girl, Billie, was a force that couldn't be stopped. Only she could show up in a low-necked evening dress, her wrists heavy with bracelets and enormous gardenias in her hair, to stand right in front of the microphone, calm and almost indifferent, without it seeming artificial. And it was only Lady's voice that could breathe new life into tired, over-repeated lyrics. As for a song as big as 'Strange Fruit', just wait and see...

'Strange Fruit' was also the source of conflict between Hammond and Billie. He knew it: he had lost his protégée. In the past, he had often repeated that she should record blues to make sure she was played on the radio, but the young girl ignored his advice. 'Your job is to please as many people as possible', he would repeat, but it didn't sink in. She didn't want to. However, when they'd met in 1931, he'd loved the cheerfulness and laughter of this young girl who was always on her way to find some fun, but who was also an extremely gifted hard worker. You got her to listen to a song twice, and she would get the lyrics spot on. You put her in the hands of a talented pianist (Willie 'The Lion' Smith, Bobby Henderson or Teddy Wilson, for example) and she would shine. And now? She drinks from the moment that she wakes up, chain smokes, jumps from one bed to another and never stops getting hammered. If only she was up to it, it would all be OK. But now she invariably arrives late for recordings or complains about going on stage. And she's become crazy about a song about... lynching! Billie must want to ruin his career – she wouldn't have chosen it otherwise. So Hammond's throwing in the towel. It's a breach of contract, of authority and his trust. It's goodbye.

Café Society

1 Sheridan Square

10 p.m. A crowd has gathered outside the Society. Billie's cab circles Sheridan Square a few times until finally Barney Josephson, the club owner, appears. A funny kind of guy, that one. And a visionary. Originally from New Jersey, they say that this well-born Jew who had previously run a shoe factory had a jazz 'revelation' at Cotton Club (142nd Street & Lenox Avenue), after which he decided to open a club. The problem was, he didn't have a clue how to go about it. It was John Hammond – again – who came to lend him a hand. On 30 December 1938, Josephson finally opened his place in Greenwich Village in a basement room that had previously been an underground bar. New York had never seen a place like it before. Its policy? Non-segregationist! With Billie on board and a well-chosen slogan ('The wrong place for the right people'), Café Society drew in 600 people a night, who came to see shows that alternated between black and white artists. And from the first evening, the puritans had to keep their mouths shut...

On Josephson's arm, Billie now makes a royal entrance into the building, while all around her people call out 'Lady! Lady Day!'. She ignores the hands that reach out and the posters plastered from the door to the foot of the staircase leading to the main room, with their capital letters: 'HAVE YOU HEARD STRANGE FRUIT GROWING ON SOUTHERN TREES SUNG BY BILLIE HOLIDAY?' That same day, these words had been stretched over a full page of *The New York Times*. Everyone in Manhattan was talking about 'Strange Fruit'. At least that's what Josephson assured her. Billie didn't stop, she was the queen, the reigning monarch of Big Apple nights, a status that brought her the respect of people from Judy Garland to Bob Hope, from Clark Gable to Merle Oberon, and even the young Frank Sinatra, who 'd been hanging around her dressing room the other night. Without success.

Oh, of course there are wagging tongues who don't like her success. Spiteful, racist and right-wing gossips for whom 'Strange Fruit' provides the perfect grounds to criticise her. 'Lady doesn't *understand* what she's singing about,' they say. 'You have to be poor and black to understand what the song means (idiots),' she answers back. A song about racism: it was a first in the United States. In actual fact, the song had been written by Abel Meeropol (using the pseudonym Lewis Allen), a white school teacher and communist party member, and was the mother of all protest songs.

Because 'Strange Fruit' mentioned what America didn't want to see or admit: its violent and racist culture, the cowardice of those who perpetuate it and the distress of those who have to endure it. Very soon, recordings of the song on 6.5mm tape cassettes would be on sale throughout the country. Ten thousand copies would be sold within the first week, even though several radio stations refused to play it. And for the moment, even if it's only the well-to-do who can go to Café Society to hear it, the words of 'Strange Fruit' reach Harlem, through word of mouth or written on scraps of paper.

'Southern trees bear a strange fruit,
Blood on the leaves and blood at the root,
Black bodies swinging in the southern breeze
Strange fruit hanging from the poplar trees.

Pastoral scene of the gallant south,
The bulging eyes and the twisted mouth,
Scent of magnolias, sweet and fresh,
Then the sudden smell of burning flesh.

Here is fruit for the crows to pluck,
For the rain to gather, for the wind to suck,
For the sun to rot, for the trees to drop,
Here is a strange and bitter crop.'

Walls that have been graffitied freely by the audience, a large ebony counter that runs down one side of the bar, pedestal tables with their chairs around them in a smoky space with no stage. Another cigarette; another drink. Billie watches the technicians that Milt Gabler has sent while they set up a heavy tape recorder as big as a fridge. It's the latest thing, apparently. In a moment, she'll be standing before the audience in a white satin dress, singing sad songs like 'I'm Gonna Lock My Heart' or 'I Love My Man'. This evening, once more, there will be young women to offer her silk scarves and French perfumes. And then, towards one o'clock in the morning, after 'What a Little Moonlight Can Do' and 'Fine and Mellow', it will finally be time for 'Strange Fruit'. In a well-oiled ritual, the lights will dim. The service will be suspended. And, with only the accompaniment of Sonny White on the piano, Billy will sing the last song of her set, before disappearing three minutes later. She'll let a gardenia fall from her hair to the floor, where it will lie for the audience to see: the only tangible trace of the presence of an artist who had already become a legend.

'Every time
I do a show
I'm up against
everything that's
ever been written
about me.'

Billie Holiday

Billie Holiday in 10 dates

7 april 1915

Birth of Eleanora Fagan in Philadelphia

1930

Starts out in Harlem clubs

1933

Meeting with the producer John Hammond and recording of her first record at the age of eighteen

1935

Collaboration with Duke Ellington in the film *Symphony in Black*, signed to Brunswick Records

1937

Friendship and collaboration with the saxophonist Lester Young Tournée and the Count Basie Orchestra

1939

Headlines Café Society, where she first sings
'Strange Fruit'

1943

Signed to Decca Records

1946

Named the Best Leading Female Vocalist by *Esquire Magazine* for the second year running

1948

Sold-out concert at Carnegie Hall

17 juillet 1959

Dies at the age of 44 in New York

Jack Kerouac

Considered one of the most important writers of the twentieth century, Jack Kerouac (born Jean-Louis Lebris de Kérouac, 12 March 1922, in Lowell, Massachusetts) was also a walking contradiction. Born to a Quebec family of Breton origin, he co-founded the Beat Generation during the 1950s along with Allen Ginsberg and William Burroughs. He also helped to redefine American mythology and sparked a revolution with one book: *On the Road* (1957). This book was a celebration of the achievement of self-fulfilment through adventure, aimless roaming, free sexuality and opiates. Although today he is widely regarded to have been one of the main inspirations of Sixties 'Flower Power', the 'King of the Beats' actually spent that decade entrenched in an angry conservatism. Labelled as racist, anti-Semitic, anti-Communist, even anti-intellectual, the author of *The Dharma Bums* (1958), *Visions of Cody* (1960) and *Big Sur* (1962) spent his final years regarded with indifference by the general public. This would only change following his death, 21 October 1969, in St Petersburg, Florida. By the time he reached forty-seven, this jazz poet, who had formerly sought out wide-open spaces, had become an obese and bitter figure who'd been living with his mother for years... Today, from Tom Waits to Bruce Springsteen, from Bob Dylan to Patti Smith, and even to a Hollywood road movie, his influence on pop culture is overwhelming.

7 p.m.

5 p.m.
Station 66
St-Lincoln Center
66th Street & Broadway

6 p.m.
Times Square
West 46th Street
& Broadway

7 p.m.
**First headquarters
of the Beat
Generation**
419 West 115th Street

5 September 1958

Station 66
St-Lincoln Center

66th Street & Broadway

That very day, exactly one year previously, Jack Kerouac had become a celebrity overnight. Just before midnight, the first copies of *The New York Times* were delivered to the kiosk on the corner of 66th Street and Central Park. The writer Joyce Glassman, his girlfriend at the time, had hung about with him to read Gilbert Millstein's column on *On the Road*. She finished with the words, '*On the Road* is a major novel.' Wow. Jack had been waiting ten years for this moment. He should have jumped for joy, but something stopped him. He didn't quite know what. In the end, all he could think about was getting drunk. Which is exactly what he'd done a short while later. Now he can't remember where his drinking session had taken him. Perhaps to the bohemian meeting places around Washington Square Park, or Pony Stable Inn (150 West 4th Street) or it could well have been Romero's (24 Minetta Lane), who knows? And then, the following day, when he'd woken up with an unbearable hangover, his name was finally on everybody's lips. Problem was, he didn't have a clue how to behave from that moment onwards.
And another problem still: now there were dozens of people who would do anything to approach him, speak to him, buy him drinks and – on occasion – kiss him. That's where things had gone wrong. The fact was that his admirers expected to meet Dean Moriarty, the hero of *On the Road*. They believed that Dean's character was based on Jack himself. But in reality his characteristics had been stolen from Neal Cassidy, the guy that Kerouac had followed about and whose 'picaresque adventures', as he called them,

he'd then recreated.

Cynical, offensive, tense, worried, drinking like a fish,
the 'King of the Beats' invariably deceived his public.
As did the press, happy to be able to fill their tabloid
columns. They asked him: Who are the Beats? What exactly
do they want? Are they going to set things alight? Not one
journalist wanted to understand that On the Road was set
in the past. At a time, not so long ago, when Rock'n'Roll
didn't yet exist. And neither did the 'youth culture', which
had come to dominate the market. Nor did anyone want to
admit that this text, which had been revised and reshuffled
over the years, was the truth. It certainly wasn't fiction.
The result: disappointed admirers who couldn't wait to get
away from this reactionary, rubicund redneck who was
something like a washed-up Gregory Peck or Alain Delon.
The media, stunned by his incoherencies, made fun of him,
behind his back at first, but later in public. He had to defend
himself. But he didn't know how. So Jack became
shameless and disorderly, talking nonsense: saying he was
anti-intellectual, pro-McCarthy, a racist. Sometimes, he got
beaten up badly for saying the wrong thing or getting
carried away over drinks. Like the time two guys had fallen
on him at the Ninth Circle Bar (139 West 10th Street).
The outcome: a fractured neck, broken arms and a
one-way journey to the nearby St. Vincent's Hospital
(203 West 12th Street).

'My whole wretched life swam before my weary eyes, and I realized no matter what you do it's bound to be a waste of time in the end so you might as well go mad.'

On the Road, Jack Kerouac, 1957

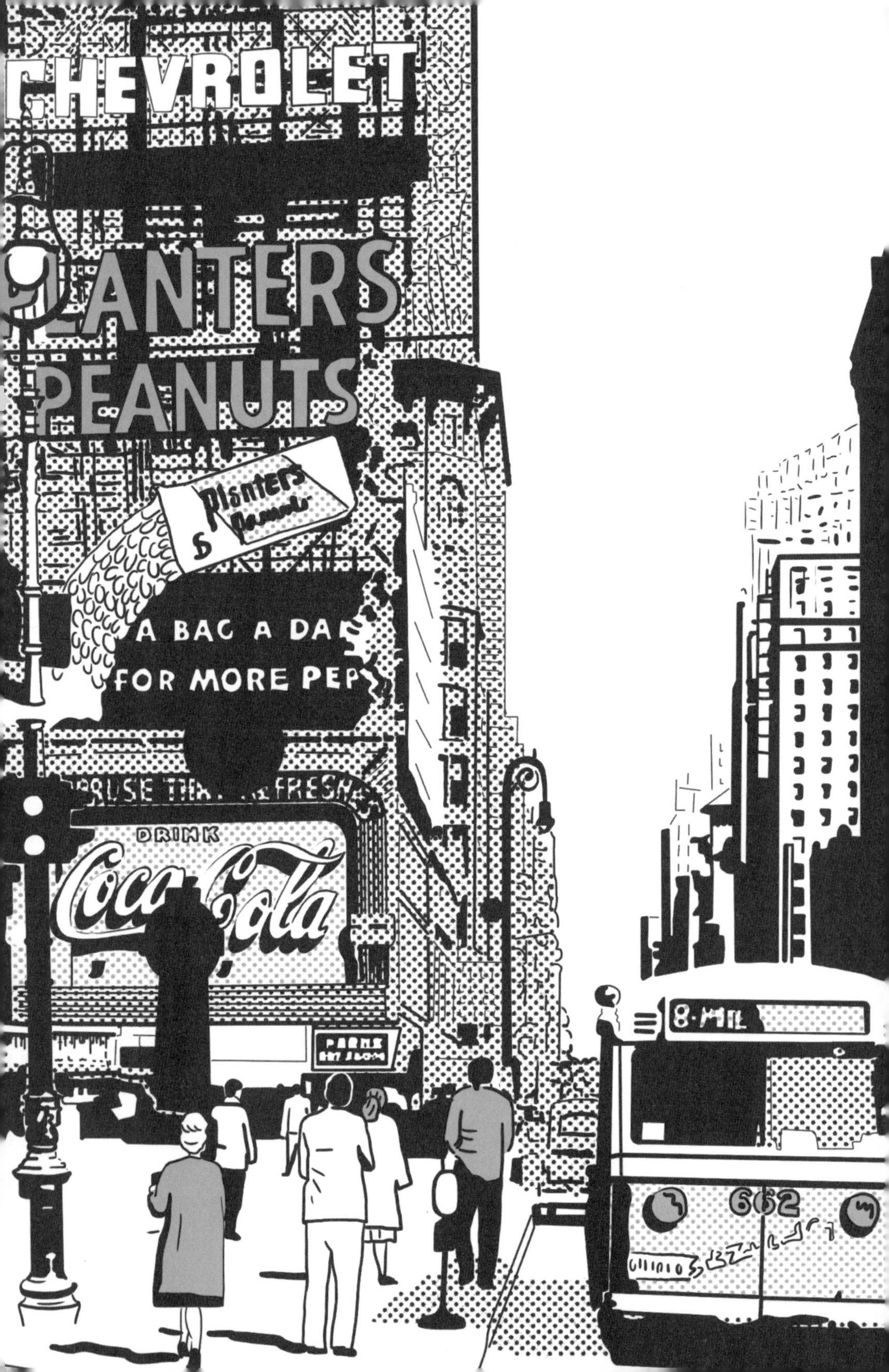
CHEVROLET
PEANUTS
FOR MORE PEP
DRINK
Coca-Cola
8-MIL
662

Times Square

6 p.m. Down Broadway, 8ᵗʰ Avenue and straight to Times Square, at the foot of the MGM cinema. Kerouac always remembers this place as it was when he discovered it in the summer of 1939. He was seventeen at the time, just a redneck who had recently arrived from Lowell, a forgotten Quebec enclave of Massachusetts where they still spoke joual. He was a talented American football player at the time. Columbia University (116ᵗʰ Street & Broadway) had taken him on, with a scholarship thrown in. One year later, a broken tibia marked the end of his sporting career. But it didn't matter. He divided his time between his three interests: writing, jazz and the prostitutes of the Theater District. He lost his virginity to one of them, a girl he had met on 46ᵗʰ Street, shortly after he arrived. Jack kept this event secret for a long time. The fact was that having been raised in a Jansenist Catholic culture where 'the body was evil' and 'an erection sent you to Hell', he feared that his harpy of a mother, Gabrielle (who he called Mémère), would make a big fuss. And arrange to bring him back, to be closer to her...

Everything had changed, here in Times Square. Nothing was as it used to be. At the beginning of the 1940s, it was the nerve centre of a self-confident nation that was getting ready to go to war. Everywhere you looked there were posters for cinemas, luxury hotels and for the fashionable restaurants or cafés favoured by celebrities. Both day and night, on 7ᵗʰ Avenue and Broadway, there was a chaos of traffic, the blaring of horns, thick clouds of fumes that turned the electric lights on Times Building blue. And covering the sidewalk was the dregs of humanity. Gangs of nutters, pickpockets, hustlers, whores, crooked cops, touts, boxers, gigolos and taxi-girls. For Jack, spending time in Manhattan meant hanging around in these places. At Pokerimo (Broadway & 44th Street), there was a room of slot machines and pinball games frequented by amphetamine addicts, which he'd rechristened Nickel-O in his book *The Town & The City*. Or otherwise, further south, at Horn & Hardart (Broadway & 14th Street), there was a cheap self-service where a plate of beans never set you back more than twenty cents. Further down, a good deal further, you had the Cedar Tavern (24 University Place), the bar where New York's artists hung out in the 1940s: Jackson Pollock and Mark Rothko got drunk there, Frank O'Hara and LeRoi Jones had endless discussions there, and the young Kerouac, proud of having joined the ranks of the *New York Telegram* and the Horace Mann Quarterly, came to sit, pretending that he was already a great writer. But what could he write about? At first, he didn't have a clue. As he had to try his hand at something, he decided on jazz. It was a logical choice: since arriving in New York he'd often spent his nights at clubs like Lenox Lounge (288 Lenox Avenue), Nick's (170 West 10th Street) or at Village Vanguard (178 7th Avenue South) where Charlie Parker, Count Base and even Lester Young played. The latter was one of Jack's heroes, as well as the guy he'd smoked his first joint with. From one all-nighter to another, in the end jazz became a kind of religion for him. Jazz made the descendent of a line of Celtic Bretons realise that he could write in the same way that jazz improvs were conjured up: all in one go! But very soon, he tired of signing articles about jazz. He needed a wider subject matter to explore. Where could he find it? His circle of friends didn't take long to provide him with it: Kerouac would study the actions of others. 'The undertaking of an author is to observe,' he would declare, much later.

'A man is beat whenever he goes for broke and wagers the sum of his resources on a single number; and the young generation has done that continually from early youth.'

The American author John Clellon Holmes on the Beat Generation, *The New York Times*, 16 November 1952

First headquarters of the Beat Generation

419 West 115th Street

The people he observed were Allen Ginsberg, William Burroughs, Edie Parker, Haldon Chase and Joan Vollmer. They were the members of an iconoclast clique that had been gathering since 1945 in an apartment down a lifeless street near Morningside Park. They had a common fondness for literature, liquor, opiates (especially Benzedrine) and a liberated sexuality. They called themselves the Libertine Circle. During endless discussions, while listening to swing and smoking dope, they imagined cultural alternatives to the conventions upheld by a rigid American society that was full of clichés and pride in its power. Just like the others, Jack got high and debated until he ran out of breath. But most of all, he listened. Perhaps he was already toying with his big project, one that would become increasingly defined as he took in every word, action and consequence. Because of his incredible memory, the others took to calling him 'Memory Babe'. But he preferred 'Ti Jean', the nickname his mother still used. Ti Jean, who passed his days propping up the bar at the <u>Angle Bar (8th Avenue & 42nd Street)</u>, and promised, along with Ginsberg and Burroughs, to write 'the truth, whatever the cost, even if it hurt', and finally, like Kerouac, was the first of the group to get published, which really just wasn't done. And although he kept it to himself, the name Ti Jean also meant the soothing respite he sought from Mémère, without any consequences, when *The Town and the City* (1950) was published

The indifference of the public, the publishing world, the critics and his friends, was just like success; it was an experience Jack wasn't prepared for. He'd even thought about giving up writing after the flop of his first novel. Only Allen Ginsberg and Joan Haverty, his second wife, had encouraged him. Was it because they were blind? Or was it politeness? He wasn't sure. Or maybe they were both counting on his incredible memory, the memory that had allowed him to remember his trips with Neal Cassady from 1947 to 1959 in such clear detail. The beautiful landscapes they'd passed through and the seedy parking lots that Kerouac described in their various shades of grey. The gloomy saloons and deserted roads that he described excellently with all the nuances of the dust.

The southerners who were always up for a fight and the quarrelsome barmen with their coarse language and accents. The whistles of trains, the roaring of motors, the banging of doors and the lights of the drowsy towns that he summoned up in all their colours.

And then the Libertine Circle slowly disintegrated. In the end, the apartment at 419 West 115th Street was left deserted. Gregory Corso, William Burroughs and Allen Ginsberg moved to a sober furnished flat at 206 East 7th Street, north of Alphabet Street in East Village. Neal Cassady returned to his brood in California. And Kerouac took himself off to mope melancholically at Mémere's place in Queens, where Joan Haverty eventually joined him.

Jack doesn't exactly remember the course of events there. Was it at Hector's (44 Little W 12th Street) or at Riviera (225 West 4th Street), They were two equally smoky, damp and dangerous bars. Anyway, on one night of drinking, he'd been discussing the lost generation with John Clellon Holmes, a close friend from his group who, at the time, wrote for *The New York Times*. 'We were trying to think of a way to describe our generation,' he recounted. 'We had thought of a few ways and I said, "It's really a beat generation!"' John leapt up and said, "That's it! It's exactly that you see..."' Is it true? Or should we give credit to Holmes's later version? 'Jack and I were talking specifically about the lost generation.

When he came up with this phrase, we never said. "That's it!", nor did we make a big fuss about it.'

In 1952, when Holmes published his book *Go*, followed by the article 'This is the Beat Generation' that was published in *The New York Times*, Ti Jean flipped, swearing to anyone that would listen, 'It's mine! I invented that name!'

9ᵗʰ Ave

W 23ʳᵈ St

8ᵗʰ Ave

12ᵗʰ Ave

9 p.m.

W 14ᵗʰ St

Hudson River

10.30 p.m.

Broadway

9 p.m.
Jack Kerouac and
Joan Haverty's
apartment
454 West 20ᵗʰ Street

10.30 p.m.
Gaslight Café
116 MacDougal Street

W Houston St

1.30 a.m.
Camino Gallery
92 East 10ᵗʰ Street

3 a.m.
Allen Ginsberg and
Peter Orlovsky's
apartment
170 East 2ⁿᵈ Street

Canal St

Broadway

Jack Kerouac and Joan Haverty's apartment

454 West 20th Street

 9 p.m.

Nowadays, the apartment where Jack Kerouac and Joan Haverty lived is a luxury loft in a residential street in Chelsea. The contemporary art galleries that, over the last two decades, have built the reputation of this neighbourhood are just a stone's throw away, as is the personal studio of the artist Jeff Koons, or the elegant West 22nd Street townhouse where Louise Bourgeois lived until her death in 2010. However, in 1951, when Joan signed the lease of a studio near 10th Avenue, this part of Manhattan, which had previously been inhabited by the Irish, wasn't at all that welcoming. It was a harsh environment populated by dockers and workers and Chelsea, at the time, was a warehouse area with the Hudson River Railroad running through it. Seven years later, Kerouac stands facing number 454 20th Street, looking at the silent windows on the second floor of the sleepy brownstone. Very little has changed here.

'Writers are, in a way, very powerful indeed,' wrote William Burroughs. 'They write the script for the reality film. Kerouac opened a million coffee bars and sold a million pairs of Levis to both sexes. Woodstock rises from his pages.'[1] This achievement took place in a modest studio with faded white walls and a matt parquet floor, where he languished, despite Joan imploring him to go out. Nothing changed until the publication of Go made him lose it. It was in this apartment that he'd re-read a 23,000-word letter he'd received several months earlier from Neal Cassady ('The greatest piece of writing I ever saw,' he declared) and decided to write his take on things. Joan asked him,

1 *The Adding Machine*: Selected Essays, William S. Burroughs, 1993

'What exactly happened with Neal?', and he replied,
'My whole wretched life swam before my weary eyes, and
I realized no matter what you do it's bound to be a waste of
time in the end so you might as well go mad.'[2]

2 *This Is the Beat Generation* New York San Francisco Paris, James Campbell, 1999

The rest of the story is common knowledge. It forms
part of the history of popular culture. First, it was Jack who
got annoyed about having to put a new page in his
typewriter each time he finished the previous one. Then, it
was Joan who brought a seven-metre roll of Japanese rice
paper back from Bill Cannastra's, a hot-headed guy who
was close to the beat group. Then, it was Kerouac who
glued the rolls together from end to end and slipped the
start of the scroll into the machine. It was Ti Jean who
wrote the first words in April 1951: 'I first met Neal not long
after my father died... I had just gotten over a serious
illness that I won't bother to talk about except that it really
had something to do with my father's death and my awful
feeling that everything was dead.' It was finally 'Memory
Babe' who, over twenty days, alternating between
Benzedrine, coffee and pea soup, wrote the first version of
a catalytic novel that made thousands of young people take
to the road in the 1960s, looking to find themselves.

Had Jack really done all of that? At this very moment,
with Chelsea enveloped in the heavy fog spat out by the
Hudson, he's not so sure. First, because on the way here he
made a detour via the Caravan Café (102 West 3rd Street)
and now he's drunk. And second, because over the last
year, he's made a great effort to hide the truth: *On the Road*
wasn't written in one go. This novel is by no means the
result of spontaneous prose. It is rather a text that was
meticulously corrected and improved before it was finally
published. But nobody knows that yet.

'It is because
I am Beat,
that is, I believe
in beatitude.'

Jack Kerouac

Gaslight Café

116 MacDougal Street

10.30 p.m. It's been a while since he was last here. And nothing has changed since the beginning of the Fifties when he used to hang out in the corner with Allen, Corso and Burroughs. There's still that same foul-mouthed guy at the door, the one who's seen you a thousand times but still eyeballs you as if you've got the wrong place, nodding at the sign behind him: 'No, your goddamned friends aren't inside.' There's still that same heavy smell of tobacco that fills the space and mixes with a smell of hay that's so strong you could've sworn there was a stable hidden in the back room. There's still the same old regulars, crooked guys, lost girls, beat beatniks, chatty intellectuals and flea-ridden folk types who spring to life when you accidentally touch their rags. Then there's the boss John Mitchell behind his counter. The poets LeRoi Jones and Diane di Prima who, from their table, bring law and order to the bar. The bard Dave Van Ronk is on stage. A few years later, a young Bob Dylan would stand in the same place. Finally, there's still the clicking fingers and the yeahs! of the audience that are the sign of a well-delivered piece of blues. But now, the neighbours are sleeping, or pretending to do so, although upon the slightest noise they threaten to call the police who can't do a thing. In short, this is the Gaslight Café in all its glory, where they would usually end up after drinking their fill at Café Reggio (121 MacDougal Street), San Remo (93 MacDougal Street) or Wha? (115 MacDougal Street). The Gas, where they would trade books by Sartre or Camus that they'd snuck from the nearby Eighteen Street Bookshop (32 West 8th Street). This book shop was run by the Wilentz brothers, and up until recently Jack had used it as a mail drop, but he hadn't returned since

copies of *On the Road* started selling like hot cakes.
You never knew, his former benefactors could ask him a
favour: he's heard that business is slow these days.
For Kerouac, helping them out wasn't an option. Not even
for old times' sake. It wasn't his style. For favours he turned
to Ginsberg and co, the suckers who still pandered to the
whims of their friend turned star. If he took advantage of
their generosity, going to one of their houses in the small
hours when he'd knocked back drinks without asking at the
others' – if they didn't mind, if he was invited, should they
begrudge him? He would spin out of control, crying 'pieces
of shit', 'dirty Jews', 'fuckin' lousy intellectuals!', and so on.
And still not one of his friends would give him the punch in
the face that he deserved. That being said, Burroughs
seemed tempted. 'Old Bill' would definitely have the guts to
smash his jaw in. In fact, since their trip together to Tangier,
Kerouac did everything he could to avoid him.

A girl comes towards him. She wants a drink. Has she
recognised him? Here, everyone knows who Jack is, although
nobody gives a damn. Except for her, the poor girl. She's
probably not from the city. She's the kind of girl who might let
herself get sucked in. So the writer launches into his tales,
talking about the port and medina of Tangier, evoking Paris,
Brittany and England, which he'd found boring. And she
listens to him with delight, all fresh, thanking her lucky stars
for having helped her to find her way out of the dump to live
up this sleepless night along with others in the Village. And
here she's met this guy who used to be handsome, but today
is worn down, sad and taking refuge in his lies. Because it's
not Kerouac who is the great traveller, but Neal Cassady.
And it's not Jack who is an adventurer, but Burroughs (and a
real one at that). Jack had never been a free man, that was
Ginsberg. In fact, whenever he leaves America, he gets
homesick. Like when he was in the Rif or Paris, Brest or
Kervoac. Away from home, everything horrified him: comfort
levels, sanitary conditions, the food. So after the trips that he
grudgingly goes on, not out of choice but give him material
for his stories, the 'Dharma Bum' inevitably returns to

Gabrielle. To Mémère. To his mum who mollycoddles him, and whom he hates. To that 'stupid, small-minded vindictive peasant, incapable of a generous thought or feeling,' as Burroughs wrote in July 1958, but who he stays with because of a promise he'd made to his dying father. Oh, the harpy who is the reason why he drinks, loathes himself and is screwing up his life.

Oh, did he say that out loud? The girl has disappeared. And silence has fallen in the café. The lights have even been switched on. And from the door, the guard dog eyes him as if he's only just recognised him...

Camino Gallery

92 East 10th Street

1.30 a.m.

From Greenwich Village, take Bleecker Street, join lower Manhattan, make a stop at the White Horse Tavern (567 Hudson Street), and then at Figaro (186 Bleecker Street). From there, turn south to arrive at Bohemia (15 Barrow Street) hidden away down a flea-ridden Greenwich street. Here, make a stop once again, remembering having seen Charlie Parker (who lived opposite) drinking there as if determined to drown himself, and Charlie Mingus barging in like a gangster. One drink. And another. Then join 10th Street via the New York Public Library (425 Avenue of the Americas) and finally arrive, staggering and by now completely hammered, at Brata Art (89 East 10th Street) and the Camino Gallery. In the winter of 1957, here, just as in the Phoenix, Area and Hansa, galleries, jazz men and poets gathered, improvising together, intertwining spoken word and beat. This blend of jazz and poetry was really Jack's thing, and he was supported by the soloists Steve Allen, Al Cohn and Zoot Sims. With them, on stage, sitting on a chair or slumped on whatever he could find when he couldn't stand any longer, he devoted himself to the 'spontaneous prose' that he'd declared himself the master of, that he swore flowed through his blood. Everyone went quiet. They listened. But in a few months, they would all read Visions of Cody, a self-absorbed novel in which Kerouac would no longer be able to distinguish between the good and the bad, the writing of a novel and the story you'd tell while drowning your sorrows at the bar...

Sometimes, however, during increasingly rare moments of lucidness, he would still achieve a stream of consciousness that 're-created the sounds of the ocean'.[3]

3 *Jack Kerouac, King of the Beats. A Portrait,* Barry Miles, 1998

'Which one?
the one?
Which one?
The one ploshed –
The ploshed one?
the same,
ah boom'

Big Sur, Jack Kerouac, 1979

'With horror
I remembered
the famous Zen
saying, "When
you get to the top
of a mountain,
keep climbing."'

The Dharma Bums, Jack Kerouac, 1958

Allen Ginsberg and Peter Orlovsky's apartment

170 East 2nd Street

3 a.m. Jack doesn't like crossing the Lower East Side. Joan Haverty lives there. Where exactly? He doesn't know. All he knows is that she is living in appalling conditions and that once a month she wages war on him trying to get him to give their daughter, Janet Michelle (nicknamed Jan), $52 maintenance allowance. But he's convinced: the girl isn't his. And he doesn't care that a court has proved otherwise with a paternity test. There's nothing to do about it. Throughout his life, the 'King of the Beats', the 'Prince of Cool' would only meet the young girl twice. Jack didn't even think about her. Ever. In many aspects, Kerouac had become an insensitive, selfish, cowardly and irresponsible figure who his friends had to house, feed, provide for and listen to. But wait? Hadn't he established himself as a successful author? As someone who had named a whole generation, and in doing so made it exist (just as F Scott Fitzgerald had given birth to the 'Jazz Age')? Above all, he was, at that moment in which he sank further into bitterness, the herald of drastic changes that nobody else could have foreseen: the replacement of the Old World by the New, in which young people seeking their ideals would invent their own lifestyles and rules. An extraordinary event. A world that was, as he would write in *The Dharma Bums* (1958) 'full of rucksack wanderers, Dharma Bums refusing to subscribe to the general demand that they consume production and therefore have to work for the privilege of consuming, all that crap they didn't really want anyway.'[5]

5 *The Dharma Bums*, Jack Kerouac, 1958

There's another ghost waiting somewhere in this poor, dirty and dangerous part of southern Manhattan: Ailene, a neurotic, mixed-race girl who could sometimes be found wandering around half naked in the middle of the night, down Paradise Alley, a cut-throat area tucked away along 11th Street. This is where the action of *The Subterraneans* (1958) takes place, a novel in which Kerouac evokes his masochistic relationship with the girl he would call 'a nutter'. Shortly afterwards, he plunged into Buddhism; was mocked by the poets Gary Snyder and Philip Whalen ('He thinks Buddha is the pope!', wrote the latter); abstained from sex (provisionally), which he saw as the cause of all his problems; and lastly, considered becoming a *bhikku* (a wondering monk). Soon after, having again returned to Mémère, Kerouac would turn to fat conservatism, rough anti-Communism, crass racism and finally, with ardent patriotism, to supporting the war in Vietnam.

Well. That's the side of Jack Kerouac we don't want to see anymore. That nobody wants to remember when, in recent years, a signed copy of *On the Road* has been bought for $4,500. And when the actor Johnny Depp has paid $5,000 for a set of souvenirs that belonged to the writer. When the automobile brand Volvo pays $20,000 to his estate for the right to cite *On the Road* in a TV advert. It's because, since the end of the Sixties, Ti Jean has become a pop culture icon, just like James Dean, Elvis and Marilyn Monroe. And his serene appearance, his American beauty, the likeable face, cheekbones and engaging smile, should stay in the collective unconscious for ever.

However, at this very moment, it's not the incarnation of cool who knocks at the door of Allen Ginsberg and Peter Orlovsky's apartment, but rather, a heavy, panting man who's completely wasted, and who yells 'Alleeeeeeen!' for them to open the door. To wake them up. But nobody answers. So the Breton hammers on the door again. He calls. And swears. And threatens. But it's all in vain. And darkness finally falls on the kid from Lowell, Jean-Louis Lebris de Kérouac, the creator of a confessional literature that enriched the American myth of the collective. The voice of a humiliated generation, to whom he would

6 *The Book of Haiku*, Jack Kerouac, 2003

dedicate this breathless haiku towards the end of his life: 'The Beat Generation is a group of kids on the road who speak about the end of the world.'[6]

'Q : What does Jack Kerouac think about Jack Kerouac?'

'A: Ah!
What do I think
about me? I'm fed
up with myself.
Well, I know I'm a
good writer,
a great writer.
I'm not a brave
man. But there's
one thing I know
I can do, that's
writing stories.
It's all!'

Jack Kerouac, interviewed on Radio-Canada, March 1967

Jack Kerouac in 10 dates

1944

Allen Ginsberg, Jack Kerouac and William Burroughs meet at Columbia, New York State

1947

Formation of the Libertine Circle in New York, a literary group that brought together Allen Ginsberg, William Burroughs, Jack Kerouac, Neal Cassady and Edie Parker

1948

Jack Kerouac uses the expression 'Beat Generation' for the first time to describe his circle of friends with the novelist John Clellon Holmes who, in 1952, published an article titled 'This is the Beat Generation' in *The New York Times*

1954

Allen Ginsberg leaves New York for San Francisco where he starts writing the poem *Howl* (published in 1956)

1954

William Burroughs settles in Tangier and starts writing *Interzone* (text that was published in 1959 titled *Naked* Lunch)

1957

William Burroughs, Allen Ginsberg, Peter Orlovsky, Gregory Corso and Ian Sommerville meet in a hotel in rue Gît-le-Cœur in Paris. There, Burroughs finished *Naked Lunch* and fine-tuned various experimental literary techniques, like the 'cut-up technique', along with Brion Gysin

1969

Jack Kerouac dies in St Petersburg, Florida. He leaves behind him a plethora of literary works consisting of novels, poems, essays, travel journals and press articles

1974

After a disastrous stay in London, William Burroughs moves to a basement flat at 222 Bowery, New York: the 'Bunker' is notably visited by Andy Warhol, Susan Sontag and Debbie Harry (Blondie). There, among other works, he writes the novels *Port of Saints* (1975) and *Cities of the Red Night* (1980)

1997

Allen Ginsberg dies in New York

2012

The film *On the Road* is released, directed by Walter Salles and featuring Viggo Mortensen, Steve Buscemi and Kirsten Dunst. The feature-length film is part of the official selection of the 65th Cannes Festival

Robert De Niro in *Taxi Driver*

Filmed in Manhattan in the summer of 1975 and released in the United States in February 1976, *Taxi Driver* propelled its director Martin Scorsese's career and firmly secured Robert De Niro's place on the cinematic world stage.

It's a brutal vision of urban paranoia and misery, written in a mere fifteen days by the screenwriter Paul Schrader, who at the time had sunk into alcoholism following a divorce. *Taxi Driver* was inspired by Fyodor Dostoyevsky's Notes from *Underground*, the personal diary of Arthur Bremer (who attempted to assassinate George Wallace, the US Democratic presidential candidate, in 1972) as well as Schrader's own decline. The film follows the story of a Vietnam veteran: Travis Bickle, a solitary young man who becomes a taxi driver in a suffocating New York. Indignant at the perversion that he sees every night, the former marine soon turns himself into a righter of wrongs, embarking on a mission to save Iris, a teenage prostitute.

Taxi Driver is a portrait of a city on the verge of bankruptcy, and can also be read as the tragic story of a New York City, once the symbol of American power, that has become an unstable Babylon. Martin Scorsese reproduces this atmosphere with hypnotic, nocturnal drives in which the stench of the city (during a heatwave, the city's garbage collectors have gone on strike) seems to be embodied by a cast of dehumanized characters.

Taxi Driver won the *Palme d'Or* in 1976 and is indisputably one of the cult films of the twentieth century. It's a film that is unsettling to watch and in which the strange finale, with its ultra-violence and improbable conclusion, continues to divide opinion.

9 a.m.

10 a.m.

W 14th St

W Houston St

West St

Canal St

Broadway

Chambers St

Broadway

6 a.m.
Robert De Niro's
apartment
88 Central Park West

7 a.m.
Charles
Palantine's rally
Columbus Circle
(West 59th Street &
8th Avenue)

7.30 a.m.
***Taxi Driver* garage**
140 West 57th Street

8 a.m.
The Show & Tell
Cinema
737 West 47th Street
& 8th Avenue

8.30 a.m.
St. Regis Hotel
2 East 55th Street

9 a.m.
Robert De Niro Sr's
former studio
Westbeth Building,
55 Bethune Street

10 a.m.
Greenwich Hotel
377 Greenwich Street

8 February 2006

Robert De Niro's apartment

88 Central Park West

 6 a.m.

On the large terrace that opens out on to Central Park, an espresso in hand, he hears sound of the front door closing. Robert's personal doctor has just left. It may have been an early visit, but it was reassuring. Apparently everything was stable and in order. The panic that had been triggered a few months earlier by a prostate cancer diagnosis now seemed to be a thing of the past. 'We got there in the nick of time,' the doc had insisted, looking for a tip. At the price he was paid, he would have to come back to get some more dollar bills. The important thing was that the matter was settled, nipped in the bud. Now he had to get ready to leave.

Grace, Robert's second wife, was still asleep upstairs. Helen and Elliot wouldn't make an appearance for another few hours yet, but his older kids still hadn't got back, a fact that annoyed De Niro. He didn't have a problem with Drena and Raphael going out to party the night away, but if they were going to get back later than 5 a.m. they were meant to get in touch. It was a signed-and-sealed deal between his elder children and him. But now it seemed that they were starting to push the limits. When they finally came back, this worried dad would have to give them a lecture, and playing the strict father wasn't really his thing. But he had no choice. If not, this behaviour would continue, and dramas could start so easily. Ever since they had all moved to this fifteen-room, $39m penthouse paid for in cash (where the neighbours included Sting and Yoko Ono), the kids had been unbearable – worse than fleas.

So, he'd have to give them a dressing down that evening.
Yep, tonight...

Even if they returned that very moment, Robert wouldn't
have time. He had a huge day ahead of him. And at some
point he would have to find the time to write something for
that night's event. He could always ask his assistant to write
a first draft and then fine-tune it. But what could he talk
about that was *fresh*? Everyone already knew everything
there was to know about *Taxi Driver*, released thirty years
ago today. The whole story behind the film was now part of
popular mythology. It could be summarized as follows:
he'd met Scorsese in the early Seventies after three minor
collaborations with Brian De Palma; he'd been cast as
Johnny Boy in *Mean Streets* (1973); and his career had
suddenly taken off when Francis Ford Coppola cast him as
a young Don Corleone in *The Godfather 2* (1974). And then,
bam! He was awarded an Academy Award for Best
Supporting Actor, and suddenly everyone wanted a piece of
him. Richard Attenborough was the first to turn up, wanting
to cast him in *A Bridge Too Far* (1977) alongside a dream cast
(James Caan, Michael Caine, Sean Connery, Laurence
Olivier...). Trying to convince him, the people from United
Artists offered him a cheque with multiple zeros.
How could he say no? But Robert turned it down, because
Scorsese had come along at the same time, a bizarre script
under his arm, in which he and Paul Schrader, an alcoholic
screenwriter suffering from his divorce, would only cast
De Niro. So, he'd taken a day to read this curious script:
the story of Travis Bickle, a lost Vietnam veteran, an
insomniac who was drowning in the solitude of New York
and decided to save a teenage prostitute he'd met in his taxi.
Dark, violent and amoral: it was the type of film that could
ruin a career. Or fast-track it; that depended. It certainly
wasn't one that would enrich you. On top of it all, Columbia
Pictures were offering a salary of $35,000, five times less
than Attenborough's proposal. And Robert's reply was, OK,
you're on! When it was released a year later in February 1976,
Taxi Driver caused fierce controversy in the United States.

'I didn't know that the characters we created in our films were existential heroes; I never studied philosophy. But I always believed in their emotions.'

Martin Scorsese, director of *Taxi Driver*

It also received the Palme d'Or that same year at Cannes, and was nominated four times at the Oscars. Shortly afterwards, having grossed more than $28m at the box office, it was considered to be a 'cult' film.

Ever since, this interesting career trajectory has been part of the legend of Robert Mario De Niro Jr, a man with a CV that Hollywood had never seen before. A breath-taking filmography (almost 100 successive films since Marcel Carné's *Three Rooms in Manhattan*, in 1965) with one hugely successful film after another. We can forgive him for the uninteresting feature-length films that came out in the 2000s. Let's face it, the actor had other interests as well. The former small-time thug from southern neighbourhoods had reinvented himself as a successful business man. Having bought and transformed the old Martinston Coffee Building in TriBeCa (TRIangle BElow CAnal Street), a Manhattan neighbourhood jammed between Canal Street and the financial district where he now owns three restaurants, a hotel, a bakery and a cinema festival, people started to call him the 'Mayor'. Although he would roll his eyes or lecture them with a smile, they (the employees, residents, suppliers, associates) insisted on it: 'Bob Mayor'!

Charles Palantine's rally

7 a.m. The driver is at the wheel, his impeccably dressed assistant by his side. Robert is in the back seat, his knees tightly tucked in, reviewing his paperwork. Outside, nothing is moving. It's been the same for weeks. You pass the 58th going south and can guarantee that you'll hit a jam. He looks outside. The car comes to a standstill on Columbus Circle, a dividing line between the Big Apple of those that have everything and those with nothing. To the north of 59th Street there are hundreds of blocks of gated residences: a luxury oasis where the super-rich live. This the world of a guy like Charles Palantine, the presidential candidate in *Taxi Driver* whom Travis Bickle gets it into his head to liquidate. His headquarters can be found a little higher up, on the corner of Broadway & West 63rd Street (nowadays a Bank of America branch). It's here that Travis meets Betsy (Cybill Shepherd), inviting her for a drink in an impersonal (West 58th Street & 8th Avenue, now the drugstore Duane Read). But things between Betsy and him would come to a sudden end. Frustrated, Travis hangs around on Columbus during the senator's rally and accosts a special agent, just for fun:

'Hey, you're a Secret Service man aren't ya? Huh?
– Just waiting for the Senator.
– You're waiting for the Senator? Oh! That's a very good answer. Shit! I'm waitin' for the sun to shine.'[1]

Could De Niro remember the Manhattan fumes of the summer of 1975 in which *Taxi Driver* was filmed? What was his reaction to the dissolute film setting? What was he like at the time? A surly and rebellious boy who had been at Conservatoire Stella Adler (31 West 27th Street) since the

[1] *Taxi Driver*, Martin Scorsese, 1976

age of sixteen, and then had attended Lee Strasberg's Actors Studio (432 West 44th Street). He was a shy and secretive boy, the only child of the poet Virginia Holton Admiral. He kept quiet about his teenage years, spent between punch-ups in the Kelmare Street gang, in this working class part of NoLIta (deriving from North of LIttle Italy). On some weekends he met his dad, Robert De Niro Sr: a quiet man and reclusive painter whose works would only achieve modest success. And that was pretty much his life. But then, *Mean Streets* (1973) brought 'Bobby Milk' (as his friends called him, thanks to his pale skin) abruptly into the limelight. Three years later, Scorsese cast him again, this time for a special take on New York. His town. A city that he would always consider to be 'the most exciting city in the world'. It was exciting certainly, but also bitter, paranoid, cruel, chaotic, violent, insomniac, lying, dirty and murderous. De Niro, who had been brought up between the Bronx, Little Italy and Greenwich Village, shared his DNA with this city. And after *Taxi Driver*, in various different films he continued to study this city's menacing, poisonous and complex nature.

'Travis Bickle is to be understood, but not tolerated.

Paul Schrader, screenwriter of *Taxi Driver*

Taxi Driver garage

7.30 a.m.

Here? Really?', the driver asks, and the assistant whines, 'But your schedule...' Robert ignores them and orders the car to stop in this road between 10th and 11th Avenue, in front of a boarded-up brick building. Now, he takes a look around while the limo has pulled to a standstill. In the 1970s, the West Side Elevated Highway rose up a few metres to the west, just before the Hudson. In this industrial environment of warehouses and garages, there are now only abandoned buildings, waiting to be the subjects of future restoration projects. Interestingly enough, apart from the racket that used to be a constant feature here, very little has changed in this former port area where *Taxi Driver* begins. It is still grimy and humid, rusty and mouldy. Thirty years ago, dressed in a khaki jacket and a checked shirt, De Niro had entered one of these garages, filled with the purring yellow taxis, which today have fallen silent, that were waiting to criss-cross the island.

The actor had visited many places like this while he was fine-tuning Travis Bickle's character. A taxi company had taken him on for a couple of months and he had really gotten into his role, even obtaining his licence. During the spring of 1975, he'd roamed the city each night, just like his character would do. He would pick up nutters, lost souls, junkies, people who were living on the edge, or who were simply abandoned. So, just like Travis, Robert experienced a 'Boschian' New York: one that was unhinged, corrupt and degraded. An abandoned and godless 'Gotham' that Bickle would wage war against: 'Listen, you fuckers, you screwheads. Here's a man who would not take it any more. A man who's stood up against the scum, the cunts, the dogs, the filth, the shit. Here's a man who stood up.'[2]   2 *Ibid*

But what exactly happened? What was it that, by the mid-1970s, had turned Manhattan into this Babel in ruins, which America viewed with a mixture of fear and embarrassment? Bruised by the race riots of the Sixties, a victim of economic stagnation and high inflation and, lastly, further weakened by high social expenditure, the town was on the verge of bankruptcy. And in 1975? Abandoned by the Ford administration, New York revealed its crumbling infrastructures, dilapidated subway, prostitution that spread from Times Square throughout the Theater District, disintegrating buildings, mountains of garbage with hobos rummaging through them looking like they've emerged from somewhere underground, its thousands of criminals and armed dealers. This scum that Travis addresses, 'All the animals come out at night – whores, skunk pussies, buggers, queens, fairies, dopers, junkies, sick, venal. Someday a real rain will come and wash all this scum off the streets.'[3]   3 *Ibid*

The former celebrated symbol of American economic and cultural strength, New York was now competing with Washington and Detroit for the title of crime capital. As Vincent Canby, editorial writer for the *The New York Times*, put it, the city was 'run by fools'. The city had become a Babylon with foul air and impossible traffic in which 'services are diminishing and the morale is such that ordering a cup of coffee in a diner can turn into a request for a fat lip.'[4]   4 *The New York Times*, 10 November 1974
The progressive movement of the 1960s had drifted off course. Fear governed everything. Previously, people had feared the sudden transformations of a town that had historically been torn apart by strong opposing forces (wealth and poverty, nationalism and mass immigration, modernity and archaism…). But now, fear wasn't merely present in people's minds – it had become visible and drove New York City's very pulse.

It was everywhere, constantly, and could be seen 'in the clusters of stores that close early because the streets are sinister and customers no longer stroll after supper for

newspapers and pints of ice cream.'[5] With *the Son of Sam*, a psychopath who had committed six murders, still on the loose, stepping into some neighbourhoods after dark meant risking certain death. Anyone who wanted to hang around on Alphabet Street at night was told 'Avenue A: You're attacked. B: Beaten. C: Cutten. D: You're dead'. This was just the type of place where Travis Bickle's taxi ventured, 'I go all over,' he swears. 'I take people to the Bronx, Brooklyn, I take 'em to Harlem. I don't care. Don't make no difference to me.'[6]

5 *The New York Times*, article written by David Burnham, 3 June 1969

6 *Taxi Driver*, Martin Scorsese, 1976

'You're dead!'

Travis Bickle, *Taxi Driver*

SHOW & TELL

| LIVE SHOW | XXRATED MOVIES |

Show & Tell

FRE

The Show & Tell Cinema

737 West 47ᵗʰ Street & 8ᵗʰ Avenue

Drive around the city at this time and you could be forgiven for having murderous thoughts. The limousine doesn't move and there's one red light after another. Tourists cross the roads any way they like and couriers cut right in front of you. And it doesn't get any better at night. Manhattan traffic doesn't die down at all nowadays. Thirty years earlier, in 1975–6, you could drive around certain neighbourhoods without worrying about being troubled by the police. It was simple: the police didn't bother patrolling areas like the Theater District and East Village.

Right now, Robert is passing through the Theater District. These days he has to make a conscious effort to remember what the north of Times Square used to be like. Today all you can see are bank branches, galleries, dozens of lounge restaurants and off-Broadway theatres. Thirty years earlier, the same buildings housed a suite of dingy diners and adult cinemas where a porno cost 50¢ a ticket, just like the Show & Tell. This was one of many places of abandon where, in *Taxi Driver*, Travis Bickle came to find solace for his loneliness in the early hours, once his shift was over. Here, he tried to catch the attention of the edgy concession girl (Diahnne Abbott, De Niro's first wife). Without success.

'Can I help you?
– Yeah, what's your name? My name's Travis.
– That's nice, what can do for you?
– I'd like to know what your name is, what's your name?
– Give me a break.
– You can tell me what your name is, I'm not going to do anything.

– Do you want me to call the manager?

– You don't have to...

– TROY!

– All right, okay, I'm just, okay, can I have Chuckles?
Do you have any jujus? They last longer.'[7]

7 *Ibid*

From there, you don't need to head much further south
to find another adult movie theatre and the setting for one
of *Taxi Driver*'s cult scenes. At 213 West 42nd Street &
7th Avenue you can see where the Lyric used to be, an old
opera school that was turned into a theatre in 1903, and then
into a family cinema following the Great Depression. It then
became an adult movie theatre in the early Seventies, and
Travis invites Betsy there to see *Sometime Sweet Susan*
(Fred Donaldson, 1975), an obscure erotic B-movie.
Horrified, this girl from the privileged parts of town flees in
a taxi, leaving Bickle on his own, unnerved and bitter on a
sidewalk on 42nd Street. 'I realize now how much she is like
the others, so cold and distant,' he complained to himself.
'Many people are like that. Women for sure. They're like a
union.'[8]

8 *Ibid*

Afterwards, the Lyric was demolished in 1994, just like
its neighbour the Apollo Cinema, to make way for the
imposing Lyric Theatre, the second largest theatre on
Broadway by seating capacity. Another building that was
razed to the ground is the Variety Theater (3rd Avenue &
East 13th Street) where Travis first met Iris (Jodie Foster), a
teenage prostitute he would later encounter at 3rd Avenue &
East 13th Street in NoLIta. A couple of blocks away,
at 204 East 13th Street, was Matthew, also known as 'Sport'
(Harvey Keitel): a pathetic pimp who Bickle would do away
with during the brutal finale. Scorsese had to remake this
scene on Columbia's orders. As it was, *Taxi Driver* would
have been classed as an X-rated film (inaccessible for
anyone aged twenty-one and under). However, it wasn't this
scene's violence that caused the most discussion, but its
confusing epilogue. Thirty years later, this curious ending
is still the subject of speculation.

St Regis Hotel

2 East 55th Street

8.30 a.m. You see, after acting so strangely with Betsy, shooting a young black man in a grocery store, trying to assassinate Charles Palantine, massacring Sport and two of his cronies and finally 'saving' Iris, Travis becomes... a hero!
There are tributes to him in the press, a thank-you letter from the kid's parents and a slate that is wiped clean by the authorities. Once recovered, Bickle returns to his taxi as if nothing had happened. Until the night when he waits outside the St Regis, a five-star hotel and one of the most expensive places in New York, where the Bloody Mary was invented. And which De Niro later visited in private. Nearby are the boutiques of De Beers and Ralph Lauren; opposite, the Sony Plaza Public Arcade; at an angle, a Presbyterian church. In this loaded part of Manhattan, Robert can conjure up the strangeness of the final scene that was shot here. Betsy suddenly emerges from the St Regis and gets into his taxi. A few short exchanges, until her stop on Upper East Side. The woman gets out. Then Bickle departs, his gaze fixed, having refused to let her pay. And ...The End! There was an outcry from the critics. In *Newsweek*, 1 March 1976, the journalist Jack Kroll wrote, 'In their eagerness to establish rich and moral ambiguities, the Catholic Scorsese and the Calvinist Schrader have flubbed their ending. It's meant to slay you with irony, but it's simply incredible.' And Scorsese would reply, 'Strange things, as we know, have happened in this city!' After that, there were more and more hostile editorials on both sides of the Atlantic until the Palme d'Or that *Taxi Driver* received in Cannes, 28 May 1976, forced the most stubborn critics to hold their tongues.

Robert De Niro Sr's former studio

Westbeth Building, 55 Bethune Street

 Right now, Robert is running late. Perhaps he shouldn't have made his way out east, on the trail of a long-distant film that people still harped on about. It felt like so long ago that he'd improvised the words 'You talkin' to me?', repeating them in different tones of voice in a bachelor's apartment that looked like it came from the end of the world. But this phrase had been so copied again and again over the decades by pop culture, it now eluded him – but at the same time, he liked it. Could he mention it in his speech that evening? Perhaps not. Too predictable. It would be better to talk about what he had seen of New York that morning. The environments that just yesterday had been apocalyptic, but today were so peaceful and calm. This energy that once had been so brutal, as if death was constantly just around the corner, but that today was soothing, almost provincial. Like here, in Greenwich Village, a neighbourhood where he'd lived as a child (at <u>219 West 14th Street</u>), on the outskirts of an area that at the time was occupied by groups of beatniks and jazzmen, high on Benzedrine, who got into scraps between the seedy bars and the broken-down clubs.

At this epicurean crossroads, which was known as 'America's bohemia' during the sixties, lived Bobby Milk's father. At the time he had resided in the Westbeth Building, a cooperative that was set up in the former Bell Laboratories Buildings in 1968 and housed various artists' studios. The photographer Diane Arbus, the composer Gil Evans and the choreographer Merce Cunningham had all had their studios here. Their visitors included Robert Rauschenberg, Andy Warhol and John Cage. Nowadays, the companies New School for Drama, LAByrinth Theater and Brecht Form are all based in the buildings. At the entrance, a concierge sits behind a metal desk.

On the wall there's a list of the residents, some of whom have never left the building since they moved in some thirty years ago. In the second column it says 'Robert De Niro Sr, app. 4F'. His son takes the bronze-wallpapered elevator. Previously, it had been a freight elevator. On the fourth floor, a pristine corridor checkered with sunlight leads to a reinforced door on the far eastern side. A turn of the key, and the son finds himself in a tired white studio in which paint stains can still be seen on the walls, the steel beams and the parquet floor. There are paintings everywhere, dozens of them. Most of them have never been exhibited.

Since his father's death in May 1993, Bobby Milk had retained the lease on this empty studio. He'd never even thought about investing it. But sometimes he lingered here on his own, sometimes just for a moment, sometimes for hours, observing, as if he'd only just discovered the oil paintings with their haunted landscapes. Here, he toyed with a large project. A project that would only come into being in 2014 with the airing of the documentary *Remembering the Artist Robert De Niro Sr* on the cable channel HBO. 'I did it for the grandkids and my young kids, who didn't know their grandfather,' he explains. 'We were not the type of father and son who played baseball together, as you can surmise. But we had a strong connection. [...] My father wasn't a bad father, or absent... He was absent in some ways, but he was very loving.' One day, once this overwhelming volume of paintings, drawings and sculptures had been archived, photographed or exhibited, the actor would maybe contemplate leaving the building. However, he quickly concedes, 'I've tried. But I couldn't do it.'

'You know uh, a man, a man takes a job, you know, and that job, I mean, that becomes what he is. You know like uh, you do a thing and that's what you are. You become the job.'

The 'Wizard', *Taxi Driver*

Greenwich Hotel

377 Greenwich Street

10 a.m. Take Seventh Avenue South to Canal Street, continue down Varick, then join western Greenwich via North Moore Street. It's a routine. Robert De Niro enters his fiefdom: TriBeCa. It's a neighbourhood that the actor knows like the back of his hand, after spending his teenage years coming here to watch lorries unload at dawn, while all around the factories slowly came to life. With its workshops, warehouses, garages and thirty-floor brick towers with who knows what inside, TriBeCa was one of the industrial hubs of the island. It was populated by workers but was abruptly deserted in the Sixties when, just like SoHo in the north, the town relocated its factories to the outskirts. A decade later, this disused area became a gloomy neighbourhood with a dangerous reputation, an unpopulated area where lawlessness ruled. And where the expansive spaces waited to one day be brought back to life.

And then? Then, TriBeCa became a reflection of the renewal of this part of Manhattan. Boho families converted former studios into luxury lofts, and De Niro, who had lived in this neighbourhood, where Jay-Z and Beyoncé, Justin Timberlake and Jessica Biel now live, for a long time, suddenly opened three restaurants there: Nobu (105 Hudson Street), Locanda Verde (377 Greenwich Street) and Tribeca Grill (375 Greenwich Street). These were joined by a bakery, TriBakery (186 Franklin Street), the offices of Tribeca Film Festival founded in 2002 and a hotel, the Greenwich, which feels like a family home. The actor now enters this hotel, along with his assistant and two guys, each carrying a De Niro Sr painting. The son would later exhibit them in the hotel. But now there were more pressing matters at hand.

'You talkin' to me?
You talkin' to me?
Well, then who the
Hell else are you
talking to?
I'm the only
one here.'

Travis Bickle, *Taxi Driver*

He had to give the orders for a party at the Locanda Verde, for which nothing had yet been organized. Wines, dishes, music, lights. Robert gave instructions in a low and neutral voice. An assistant took notes. Another arrived with some papers, then disappeared. He really should take a look at that evening's speech. Now, or maybe later. But he didn't fancy writing anything. So perhaps he would improvise, say that he was celebrating New York. What this city had been, what it had come through and what it had retained from the past – and how it reacted towards anyone who tried to seduce or dominate it. That was the subject of a song that he had sung into the eyes of Liza Minnelli (*New York, New York*, 1977). After having portrayed Johnny Boy, Vito Corleone and Travis Bickle – and before playing Jack LaMotta, Noodles Louis Cyphre and Al Capone – this time De Niro was Jimmy Doyle. A *Doppelgänger*. Both his double and at the same time another person. A gifted, small-time thug who had grown up in America's cultural gaps, but who, the moment he started acting or reciting, felt his sadness seeping away slowly, finally disappearing. And setting him free.

Taxi Driver in 10 dates

1972

Paul Schrader writes *Taxi Driver* in two weeks, with a revolver constantly by his side

1974

After considering Brian de Palma, Columbia Pictures chooses Martin Scorsese to direct the film

Summer 1975

Taxi Driver is filmed in Manhattan

24 December 1975

Death of the composer Bernard Herrmann, the day after the film's original soundtrack is recorded

8 February 1976

The film is released in the United States, it grosses $28.3m for an initial budget of $1.3m

1976

It is awarded the Palme d'Or at Cannes and receives four nominations at the Oscars

1981

John Hinckley Jr makes an assassination attempt on President Ronald Reagan and confesses to having copied Travis Bickle

1994

Taxi Driver is chosen to be preserved in the American Library of Congress's National Film Registry

2005

The magazine *Time* chooses *Taxi Driver* as one of the one hundred best films of all time

2010

Robert De Niro and Lars von Trier announce that they will team up for a remake of *Taxi Driver*

Andy Warhol

Andy Warhol, artist, director, producer, screenwriter, photographer, but also publicist, actor, presenter and businessman, whose real name was Andrew Warhola Junior, is a titan of American pop culture.

Born in Pittsburgh on 6 August 1928 to Slovak parents, he studied at the Carnegie Institute of Technology (motto: 'Working is praying') from 1945–8. He then became a commercial artist in New York, notably working for *Glamour*, *Vogue* and the *New Yorker*. First, he created paintings inspired by comics, then he joined the American Pop Art movement after discovering Roy Lichtenstein's work at the Leo Castelli gallery. Warhol's work, which was characterized by a fascination for mass consumption, would stigmatize the standardization of consumer products like Campbell and Coca-Cola. He soon applied the same approach to pop culture celebrities like Marilyn Monroe and Elvis Presley.

Warhol was a shrewd businessman as well as a socialite, and in 1963 he created the first Factory, an industrial space envisioned as an artistic production workshop and the epicentre of underground activity, in which high society and freaks could come together under one roof. Regular visitors included Truman Capote, Tennessee Williams, Bob Dylan, Salvador Dalí and The Velvet Underground.

Warhol was shot and wounded in 1967 by the feminist Valerie Solanas and consequently gave up painting to dedicate himself to his film work, which was both radical and experimental. He returned to painting at the beginning of the Seventies and continued his exploration into the pathologies of the American Dream over the following decades. Andy Warhol died in New York on 22 February 1987, leaving behind him a significant body of work characterized by powerful insights, one of which was the importance that consumer society places on image.

Hudson River

W 14th St

W Houston St

Canal St

Broadway

11 p.m.

Chambers St

Broadway

9 p.m.
Factory III
860 Broadway

9.30 p.m.
Union Square
Union Square East
& East 17th Street

10 p.m.
Jean-Michel
Basquiat's loft
57 Great Jones Street

10.30 p.m.
CBGB & OMFUG
315 Bowery

11 p.m.
Underground
Cinematheque
80 Wooster Street

12 a.m.
Electric Circus
– The Dom
19–25 St. Mark's Place

1985

Factory III

860 Broadway

The rooms of Factory III are empty, and Andy hates the silence. He tries to avoid being on his own as much as possible. When he finds himself alone, the anxiety starts eating away at him, like this evening. And his taxi number isn't answering. That's another thing that upsets him – there's no way he can walk all the way to East 66th Street. There's nobody waiting for him there, not that he knows of. Apart from the cats his mother left behind. He doesn't know how they survive, they just keep on going. That's another thing that annoys him. But if he doesn't go home, where should he go?

He glances outside, taking care to hide himself within the velour curtains. A gunshot can happen so easily and he knew it well. How could he forget? It had happened just ten years ago in front of his current office. At 33 Union Square West, where the second Factory had been on the fifth floor. At the time, Warhol dreamt of a Hollywood career. He had gradually stopped painting, had surrounded himself by his group of freaks and shot impenetrable films, which were on the whole misunderstood: *Chelsea Girls, Super Boy, Lonesome Cowboys,* and so on. Then, 3 June 1968, she burst into his life. Valerie Solanas, a militant feminist with a dubious past (prostitution, drugs) who, like so many other lost souls, had become a regular at the Factory. A few months later, she had founded SCUM (*Society for Cutting Up Men*). This had piqued Andy's curiosity, but not for long, it hadn't lasted.

However, Valerie Solanas had taken his distant curiosity

for real interest. It was too late: she gave him a manuscript
of her play, *Up Your Ass*, and he was unable to refuse.
It was a play about a destitute prostitute who hated men.
As often happened, Andy hadn't followed up. It seemed
that the original manuscript had been lost. He excused
himself, and to make up for it gave the girl a minor role in
two dud films. But that didn't calm Solanas. On 3 June 1968,
she waited for him in the hall of 33 Union Square West.
Next thing, there were three bullets in Andy's chest.
He had a narrow escape; the bullets went through his lung,
spleen, stomach, liver and oesophagus. *Time* had a field
day: 'Americans who deplore crime and disorder might
consider the case of Andy Warhol, who for years has
celebrated every form of licentiousness [...] The pop-art
king was the blond guru of a nightmare world,
photographing depravity and calling it truth.' It's interesting
that they wrote it in the past tense...

'We try to last
more than we try
to live.'

Andy Warhol

And afterwards? 'I've been stitched so much that I'm like a Dior dress,' Andy said jokingly to anyone who'd listen. He had to wear a surgical corset every day, which he had fun painting. It itched and annoyed him – him, Warhol! He had to focus on a new piece for the series *Skulls* that he'd started in 1968 and would soon finish. But the contraption pressed against his kidneys and it was all he could think about. The telephone didn't ring. Maybe he should wait a while. And in the meantime, mechanically prepare another 'Time Capsule': one of the cardboard boxes that he filled each week with various personal objects (photos, drawings, bills, shirts, magazines, etc.), which an assistant would then seal, date and place in the basement. It'd been ten years since he'd started them. And now there were hundreds of identical packages in the basement, waiting to be sold one day like party bags.[1] The problem was, how much to charge? $2,000 a box? $4,000? More? He had no idea.

1 610 Time Capsules, of which less than a quarter have been opened, are at the Andy Warhol Museum in Pittsburgh

Union Square

9.30 p.m. Under his silver wig, Andy carries a handkerchief that once belonged to his mother, Julia Warhola, and on which there's one of the religious symbols she used to stitch into his clothes as a child. He looks around him fearfully, rooted to the spot, like a lost little boy: Union Square with its groups of tourists hurrying who knows where, the businessmen jostling around the subway entrance, the bums squabbling over a bench, and the greasy scraps of paper that litter the ground or swirl on the wind. A drifter hammers away at a bongo drum. And there's no taxi in sight. To find one, he would have to cross the park to East 14th Street. Perhaps he would have more luck there. But then again, where could he go? The thought of going to a restaurant or a party on his own didn't even cross his mind. It had always been his golden rule. Oh! Before, there had always been one of his Superstars or a freak from his group ready and willing to join him. He used to have power over other people. And he used it, dominating his creatures and using them until they became messed up, as Edie Sedgwick said – she was always so spiteful, that one. But recently he's been left deserted. That's probably the price you pay when, like Andy, you trade in the bestialization of poor souls over thirty years. As proof, the monthly Botox parties he hosts aren't as busy as they used to be. And also, now he has to woo celebrities to get them to part with their money for one of his Polaroids. Not so long ago, people were queuing up for the honour of having their portraits taken by Andy. Now, it was his turn to struggle to 'make money from the American Dream'. The result was that two long decades after having launched

his career imitating brand logos, Warhol shot TV adverts
for Burger King and TDK to maintain his lifestyle.
And to pay for his offices. Now there's a branch of Petco,
the pet food chain, above the old Factory. Andy would have
appreciated it. Perhaps he would even have agreed to
appear in an advert for the dog food brand *Natural Balance*,
an advert in which he wouldn't have said a word and in
which nothing would have happened. This would have
emphasized the great 'nothing'. 'Nothing', or eternity.
'I broke away from Dada and from myself as soon as
I understood the implications of *nothing*,' proclaimed
Tristan Tzara. '*Nothing* is exciting,' added Andy. '*Nothing* is
perfect. *Nothing* is sexy.' And here, finally, a taxi arrived.

'I want to be
a machine.'

Andy Warhol

Jean-Michel Basquiat's loft

57 Great Jones Street

 10 p.m. 'Jean' has been sulking for weeks. And for Andy, it's heartbreaking. They had told each other how they felt all right, the first accusing the second of having manipulated him, the second defending himself, saying that nothing had been arranged. The joint exhibition at the Bruno Bischofberger's gallery in Zurich had been a flop. His comeback in September at Tony Shafrazi (163 Mercer Street) had been widely criticized. Previously, the same critics had labelled Warhol as the 'ultimate philosopher of the society of the spectacle'. But now, they struck out at him, calling him, 'hot air', 'void' and 'an unremarkable and decadent *zeitgeist*'. Jean-Michel Basquiat became convinced that Andy was using his reputation to relaunch his career. And nothing had changed since then. The large canvases *Felix the Cat*, *Untitled* (*Arm and Hammer II*) and *6.99* hadn't even sold and were still in storage.

The taxi stopped on the corner of the Bowery, opposite 57 Great Jones Street: a two-storey building that Andy had been renting to Basquiat since the beginning of the year. For Jean, this arrangement only provided advantages. A work space on the ground floor and a studio on the first floor. And opposite, there was Great Jones Café (54 Great Jones Street), a Tex-Mex place that the artist routinely visited. They say that one day he left a full sketchbook by way of a tip. Further down lives his friend Glenn O'Brian, the former editor-in-chief of the magazine *Interview*, which was founded by Andy Warhol. Basquiat often dropped by at his house, scribbling away in a corner before suddenly leaving without a word and leaving his drawings behind him.

Andy tried the doorbell, but there was nobody home at

Basquiat's. And the taxi had already left. What an idiot, he'd told him to wait. Now what was he going to do?

Continue south along the Bowery until no. 222 where the poet John Giorno lived? This was his former lover and friend who had acted in his first film (*Sleep*, 1963). But John wouldn't want to go out. That being said, why didn't he knock on the door of William Burroughs' 'The Bunker' in the basement of 222 Bowery? 'Old Bill' rarely objected to an honest proposal. But which? The author of *Naked Lunch* liked paid-for sex. This did very little for Andy, who still clung to his virginity. On the other hand, he could just watch. That's what his sexuality had always boiled down to: voyeurism. But today, Andy didn't feel like it. And even if he changed his mind, he would have to venture all the way to the Bowery to get to 'The Bunker', a journey that, at this time of night, didn't come without risks. In fact, this corner of East Village was one of the most dangerous places in America. And as we know, Warhol preferred the world of airports, Valium, Russel Stover chocolates, 'empty and stupid Hollywood', white on white and the parties (these 'social diseases'). Never danger.

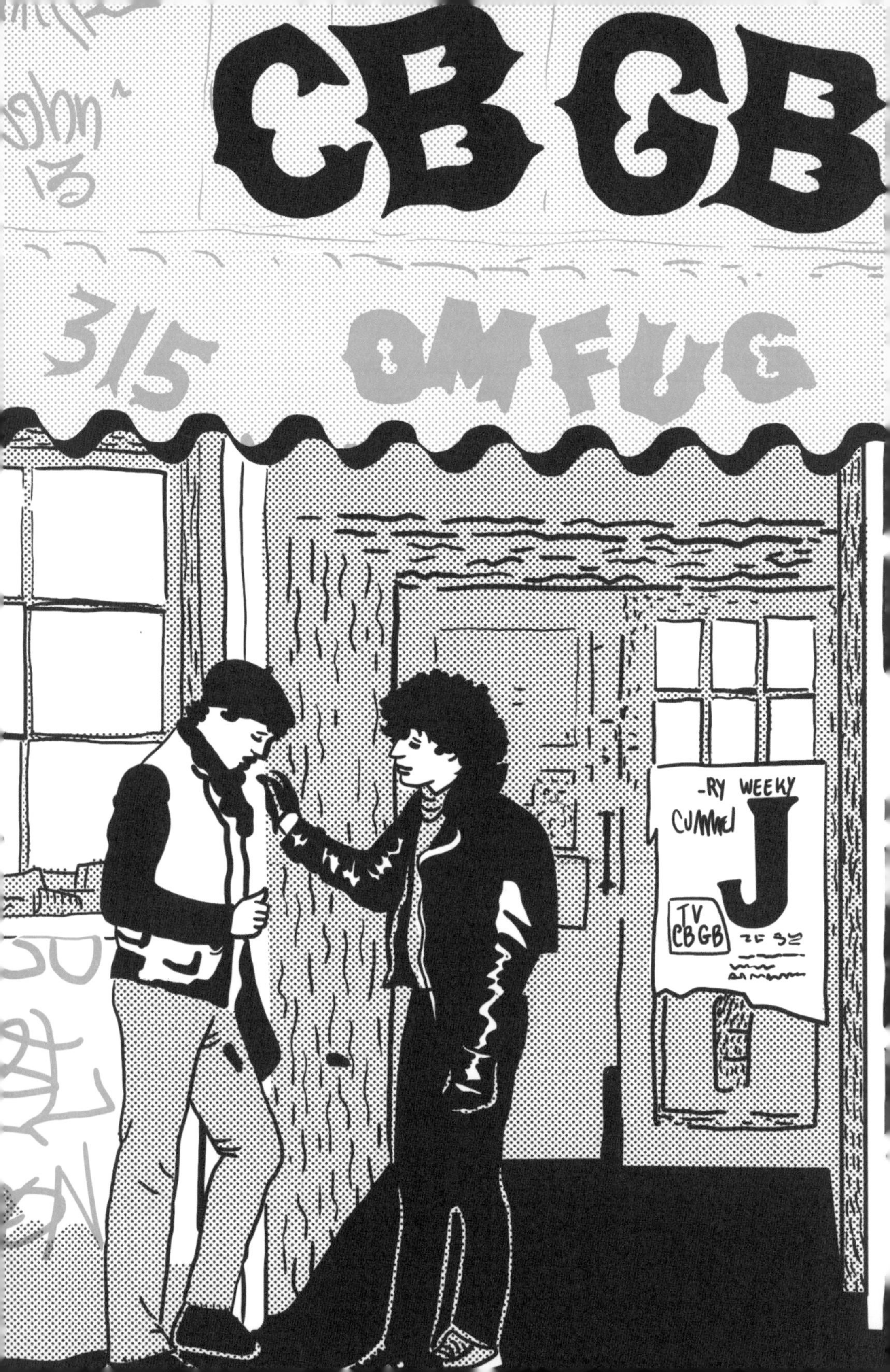
CBGB
3/5
OMFUG
-RY WEEKY
J
TV CBGB

CBGB & OMFUG

315 Bowery

10.30 p.m. Nowadays, if you hang around the Bowery you will see signs for trendy cafés and restaurants, contemporary art galleries and the elegant lines of the New Museum. You can guarantee that nothing will happen to you there. Not even at night. This part of Manhattan is now synonymous with Boho families and hip tourism. In fact, it's a neighbourhood just like any other: pleasant, cosy. However, while Andy chanced it at dusk searching for a taxi, there was a reasonable risk of getting into trouble. And going even further back into the past, when New York City was succumbing to bankruptcy in the 1970s, coming here after darkness meant almost certain death by a weapon of your choice: 1) knife, 2) baseball bat, 3) bike chain, 4) gun...
The East Village symbolized the disintegration of the Big Apple and competed with Washington, Baltimore and Detroit for the title of crime capital. It was a neighbourhood in which heroin was rife and groups of junkies loitered in doorways, completely wasted. To the south of 14th Street, tramps in unimaginable states gathered, trembling, cooked, half dead already, around braziers grouped by the dozen on street corners. At the time, the Bowery was a nightmare vision of people turning crazy, lost teenagers and male and female prostitutes wrecked on dope. Their only horizon: unsanitary, abandoned buildings, boarded-up bungalows and shady warehouses where runaway teenagers ran wild.

Now put yourselves in the shoes of a fifteen- or eighteen-year-old and admit it: where would you rather live? Take 1974, for example (the year in which Andy sealed the first of his 'Time Capsules'). This had been a great year, if you weren't bothered by the omnipresence of crime, drugs and grimy poverty, because the end of this decade marked the very moment at which disco reached its peak, a gritty rock scene was emerging from the shadows and the echoes of a new movement that was about to explode were heard from the pocket of misery that was South Bronx.

Andy hadn't experienced any of these events. He'd hardly been to the CBGB, in front of which he currently stood. This place had witnessed the very beginnings of punk rock in 1974. As a sophisticated voyeur, he'd feasted on the details that people had told him about this repulsive place: its floor full of dog shit, the seats stinking of stale beer, chilli con carne flavoured with the Dead Boys' sperm, toilets from the middle ages... Later on, Andy would venture over the threshold of 315 Bowery, escorted by his clique of course. Within the close circle of insiders (the '500'), who braved the dangers of south Manhattan to come and listen to Patti Smith, Talking Heads, Alan Vega and Wayne County, he briefly enjoyed the noisy circus that surrounded him. These grimy-looking young people from modest backgrounds and broken families sincerely thought, with a touching naivety, that by coming together around barbed riffs, cans of beer and bags of heroin, they were truly staging a rebellion. It amused him for one night. Or maybe even two. And then the 'pope of Pop Art' returned to the glamour of Studio 54 Studio 54 (254 West 54th Street), or then to the underground decadence of Mudd Club (77 White Street). But what should he do now? A taxi drew up in front of the CBGB and Andy finally escaped the bare-faced curiosity of the young people waiting opposite 315 Bowery. '80 Wooster,' he said to the driver. On the radio, Chaka Khan belts out 'I Feel for You'.

Underground Cinematheque

80 Wooster Street

For any tourist who found themselves down Wooster Street in the mid-1980s, SoHo already displayed the charm that, a decade later, would convert the former industrial heart of Manhattan into something resembling an open-air shopping centre. However, 20 years earlier, nobody would have contemplated walking the streets there, neither by day nor by night. This was down to the fact that all there was to see in 'South of Houston' was a series of abandoned warehouses, interrupted only by Canal Street.

Since the 1940s, when the first New York factories were relocated to the outskirts, the warehouses and textile factories with their cast-iron façades had remained, waiting to be demolished. In this ghost neighbourhood, full of empty, cheap spaces, 80 Wooster Street was born, a place that would help to promote marginal artistic movements. In 1962, the Lithuanian director Jonas Mekas set up the Film-Makers' Cooperative there with 23 film-makers, a distribution network dedicated to independent American cinema. In a large space with a basement in which George Maciunas, the founder of the artistic movement Fluxus, had lived, 80 Wooster Street hosted Philip Glass's first concerts, Richard Foreman's experimental plays and Yoko Ono's performances, as well as works by the choreographers Trisha Brown and Lucinda Childs. Audience members included Robert Frank, Merce Cunningham, John Cage, Robert Rauschenberg, John Lennon, Salvador Dalí and...

Andy Warhol, who received his film education there, met future collaborators (Paul Morrissey, Gerard Malanga, and so on) and convinced Jonas Mekas to work as the cinematographer for *Empire* (1964).

Ten years after the adventure started at 80 Wooster, SoHo had the biggest artist community in the United States. Among it there were painters and sculptors working on large-scale works who were already using industrial-style production techniques in bare, decaying lofts. As it was dynamic, cheap and full of spaces waiting to be claimed, the neighbourhood soon saw the opening of the collective Fluxus's ephemeral boutique (359 Canal Street) and the 'anti-restaurant' FOOD (127 Prince Street) co-founded by the artist Gordon Matta-Clark. And other multidisciplinary venues soon followed shortly afterwards: The Kitchen (59 Wooster Street), The Alternative Museum (17 White Street), White Column (112 Greene Street), Center for New Art Activities (93 Grand Street).

Few of these places still remain today. Under pressure from developers, in 1973 the mayor John Lindsay finally agreed to deregulate the property laws that were in force. As a result, the rents rose sharply and the gentrification of SoHo began. In just a few months the whole cultural fabric had been swept aside, with well-off individuals appropriating the lofts that penniless artists had been forced to abandon. All around, luxury shopping centres and pretentious boutiques and restaurants started materializing. SoHo changed into an open-air shopping centre. 80 Wooster Street, a symbol of the underground SoHo of the Sixties, became a cashmere jumper shop. Perhaps this time, Andy wouldn't have been so amused by the irony.

Electric Circus – The Dom

 12 a.m. From here, it's about a 20-minute walk to arrive at Warhol's old night-time stomping ground. Going back towards East Village, then veering north on Lafayette Street or 2nd Avenue, thirty years of clubs, bars, galleries or alternative spaces offer what remains of their gates and shop fronts. There was Café Bizarre (106 West 3rd Street), where the film-maker Barbara Rubin had seen the Velvet Underground before bringing them to the Silver Factory (231 East 47th Street). Then there was Max's Kansas City (213 Park Avenue South), where Andy liked to hang and Lou Reed and John Cale got drunk. Here you could find the very best of New York artists (Robert Rauschenberg, Roy Lichtenstein, Richard Serra), the Beat crowd (Allen Ginsberg, William Burroughs) and the new Manhattan heralds of rock (New York Dolls, Patti Smith, Debbie Harry and later on Bruce Springsteen).

Further north still, on the edge of Upper East Side, there was Sokol Hall (420 East 71st Street), a gymnasium that had been founded by the Czech and Slovak communities, where Warhol would launch the 1967 album, *The Velvet Underground & Nico*. The evening had not been a success. From here there's no reason to go further north, there's nothing there. So why not wait there, on the edge of St Mark's Place, over which St Mark's Church-in-the-Bowery (131 East 10th Street) quietly presides? In 1971, the translator Paul Blackburn inaugurated his Poetry Project there.

Andy Warhol had sometimes attended, yawning and sniggering to himself.

The taxi stops in front of 19–25 St Mark's Place.

Warhol gets out. All around him, unsurprisingly, are the bustling herds of tourists.

Shabby boutiques sell their junk. Mediocre Italian restaurants push their menus on passers-by. And what, from 1966–7, had been the Electric Circus – The Dom now houses the shelves of a Chinese supermarket! So Andy goes in, wandering down the synthetic-floored aisles filled with condiments and fresh vegetables, trying to conjure up the stage where the Velvet had played in 1966 during the *Exploding Plastic* Inevitable show, the bar in the corner where Lou Reed caused scandals over who knows what, the metal tables lined up like soldiers where Nico would write, and the platform where Malanga, Morrissey and the Superstars clique would gossip. On the eve of the Flower Power movement, a new culture club was coming into being here that nobody had given any importance to. Just opposite, in what was then the Bridge Theater (4 St Mark's Place), nobody realized that the futures of both spoken word and cinema were in play when Jonas Mekas showed Jack Smith's film *Flaming Creatures* in 1963 (and consequently spent time in jail for it), or that LeRoi Jones and Diane Di Prima would violently shake up poetry. Since, the place has successively been turned into Limbo, a shop selling hippy clothes, and then Trash & Vaudeville, where they still sell punk clothes at a good price.

'Business art is the step that comes after art. I started as a commercial artist and I want to finish as a business artist. After I did the thing called 'art' or whatever it's called, I went into business art.'

Andy Warhol

Hudson River

W 34th St

9th Ave

W 23rd St

8th Ave

12th Ave

12.30 a.m.

W 14th St

W Houston St

Broadway

12.30 a.m.
El Quijote
226 West 23rd Street

1.30 a.m.
Andy Warhol's
childhood home
1342 Lexington Avenue

El Quijote

226 West 23rd Street

12.30 a.m. Andy doesn't like eating by himself. But here he is, sitting in an alcove at the back of El Quijote, a Spanish restaurant that isn't known for the quality of its food. The walls are covered with ochre mosaics. There are black-and-white tiles on the floor. The heavy, twisted cast-iron lights in every corner of the room and pale blue lights create a strange atmosphere. Lastly, for anyone who hadn't twigged, Don Quixote is everywhere: in paintings, prints, sculptures, and even the elegant lettering etched into the dishes filled with paella. There was no question about his order. As far back as he remembers, Andy has never ordered anything but the paella, when he used to come here with Allen Ginsberg, William Burroughs, Bob Dylan or Edie Sedgwick. The first time had been in the summer of 1966, when he was filming Chelsea Girls at the neighbouring Chelsea Hotel (222 West 23rd Street). 'You're a subspecies, my dear. You're not even a vegetable!'[2]

2 *Chelsea Girls*, Andy Warhol and Paul Morrissey, 1966

The film was released on 15 September 1966, and remained his only box-office success. Just imagine – he'd made 68 feature-length films (independently or in collaboration) and had only had one commercial breakthrough! But since he released such odd films, preferring monotony to narration, and observing his actors as if they were insects; who was going to be crazy about these works in which he sought pure presence with improvisations and performances? The films were repetitive works in which people talked about God, drugs, sex, art... For *Chelsea Girls*, which was 3¼ hours long, he'd been lucky enough to have been threatened with censorship. The perfect publicity! In November 1967, the critic William

Rotsler's reaction had been, 'There's a New Kind of Film: The Underground Movement.' But nowadays, where was Nico? Damaged and fallen off the radar. And Gerard Malanga? Angry and resigned. Eric Emerson? Penniless at 29 years old. Edie Sedgwick? She'd committed suicide at 28. Perhaps she'd been right when she'd called him a vampire. He'd been using them all for 30 years now. He took everything, and only on rare occasions gave something back, provided that his side of things was kept up, and that cash kept flowing into the 'Warhol machine'; provided that his time to be declared a 'has-been' was postponed for a little longer. And lastly, provided that the shadow of illness was kept at a distance. And well, in the end, all of that exhausted him, created an emptiness, led to awful evenings like this one, in which there was nobody left to listen to him, accompany him and maybe even console him. In which everything was 'nothing'. Even Warhol himself had become a depersonalized body. A 'John Doe'. An emptiness.

Andy Warhol's childhood home

1342 Lexington Avenue

 1.30 a.m. Should he go back home, to East 66th Street? He didn't want
to. Not right away, at least. All that waited for him there was
a quiet apartment filled with bronze trinkets and lead
statues. Only expensive carpets, silk cushions, a canopy
bed, rococo lamps that did nothing to brighten the
darkness, piles of subscription magazines and the cats that
pissed where they like while their owner was out.

3rd Avenue, then. Blocks passed by on either side:
68th, 74th, 80th Street, and they stopped at 89th. Along
Lexington Avenue, on the corner of Emmelle boutique,
a purple porch marks the entrance to number 1342.
There's no need for a key. You've always been able to waltz
in here as you please. Specifically, 'always' meaning since
1959, when Warhol and his mother had moved to this
neo-Renaissance *brownstone*. At the time, he was a designer
for a theatre company and had just had his first exhibition at
the Bodley Gallery, the only one that Julia had ever come to.
Shortly afterwards, her son played a part in the launching of
the Pop Art movement in America with
Lips Stamped, a series of scarlet and pink lips floating as if
they were suspended. It was said that Mrs Warhola, with
her grey bun, stooped silhouette and country ways, may
have been the author, of this piece and the drawings that
would earn her son the title the 'Leonardo da Vinci of the
shoe trade', as coined by *Women's Wear Daily*.

And he had become successful. He'd led a studious life
on the five floors of 1342 Lexington, with the 25 cats that
were constantly tripping people up (whose offspring can
still be found in the neighbourhood today).

There was the staggering number of pieces of furniture and trinkets. The pile of canvases, acrylic paints, inks and stencils, some of which had been used to produce works like *80 Two Dollar Bills, Front and Rear* (1962) and *129 Die in Jet!* (1962). And there was Julia who, all of a sudden, would bellow, 'I am Andy Warhol!' with her thick accent that embarrassed her younger son. He had relegated her to the basement and had paid her short daily visits, giving her $55 in cash a week. In November 1972, when she died in Pittsburgh, Andy paid for the funeral, but didn't attend.

Did he ever think about his childhood? He'd been a beloved son, born pale and premature, and had grown up with nervous disorders. In the basement, he faces a metal door. Not far behind it he hears the muffled sounds of a television, the cries of children and domestic noises. Around him is the cool marble hall with green faded walls, where anyone who pauses for a moment can read a graffiti that's been left: Less Than Zero. It's the title of a successful book that had been published that very year.[3] Its author, incidentally, had copied Warhol, but never mind that. *Who* had scrawled that? Billy Name, or one of those nutters?

He didn't have a clue. And there was no use starting to panic right now. The corset was bothering him. And he could hear the sound of the taxi outside. So Andy left 1342 Lexington Avenue, soon discovering a plastic bag with Chinese lettering and a coloured logo on his arm, which he couldn't remember having held on to.

3 *Less than Zero*, Bret Easton Ellis, 1985

'If you want to know all about Andy Warhol,' he replied to his critics, 'just look at the surface of my paintings and films and me, and there I am. There's nothing behind it.'

Andy Warhol

Andy Warhol in 10 dates

Born in Pittsburgh, Pennsylvania

First exhibition at the Hugo Gallery in New York

Exhibition of *Campbell's Soup Can*, creation of *Marilyn Monroe* and *Elvis Presley* screen prints, solo exhibition at the Stable Gallery

Release of his first film, *Sleep* (a still frame of five hours and twenty-one minutes of the poet John Giorno sleeping)

Exploding Plastic Inevitable events, production of *The Velvet Underground & Nico* album released the following year

1968

Relocation of the Factory to 33 Union Square

3 juin 1968

Assassination attempt by Valerie Solanas

1969

Launch of the magazine *Interview* created with
Gerard Malanga

1985

Joint exhibition with Jean-Michel Basquiat in Zurich and
New York

22 February 1987

Dies at the age of 58 in New York

Goodies

Billy Holiday

5 cult songs by Billie Holiday
'Summertime', 1936
'Strange Fruit', 1939
'God Bless the Child', 1941
'Don't Explain', 1944
'Crazy He Calls Me', 1949

5 homages to Billie Holiday
Nina Simone's cover of 'Strange Fruit' (1965)
Diana Ross plays Billie in the film *Lady Sings the Blues* (1972)
U2 dedicate their song 'Angel in Harlem' to Billie Holiday (1988)
Etta James releases the album *Mystery Lady: Songs of Billie Holiday* (1994)
In 2011, Billie Holiday is inducted into the National Women's Hall of Fame (Seneca Falls, New York State)

Jack Kerouac

5 signature books of the Beat Generation
Go, John Clellon Holmes, 1952
Howl and Other Poems, Allen Ginsberg, 1956
On the Road, Jack Kerouac, 1957
Gasoline, Gregory Corso, 1958
Naked Lunch, William Burroughs, 1959

5 records released by the Beat Generation
Poetry for the Beat Generation, Jack Kerouac and Steve Allen, 1958
Blues & Haikus, Jack Kerouac, Al Cohn and Zoot Sims, 1958
Call me Burroughs, William Burroughs, 1965
Break Through in Grey Room, William Burroughs, 1976
Holy Soul Jelly Roll: Poems & Songs, Allen Ginsberg, 1994

Robert De Niro

5 Martin Scorsese films
with Robert de Niro

Mean Streets, 1973

New York, New York, 1977

Raging Bull, 1980

Goodfellas, 1990

Casino, 1998

5 works that quote *Taxi Driver*

Epidemic, Lars von Trier, 1987

Back to the Future 3, Robert Zemeckis, 1990

'The Badge', Pantera, 1993

La Haine, Mathieu Kassovitz, 1995

The Adventures of Rocky and Bullwinkle, Des McAnuff, 2000

Andy Warhol

5 cult films by Andy Warhol

Sleep, 1963

Empire, 1964

Chelsea Girls, 1966

The Velvet Underground & Nico: A Symphony of Sound, 1966

Lonesome Cowboys, 1968

5 cult works by Andy Warhol

Campbell's Soup Cans, 1962

Ten Lizes, 1963

Big Electric Chair, 1967

Mao, 1972–1973

Skulls, 1976

30 cult novels about New York

The American Scene
Henry James, 1907

The Age of Innocence
Edith Wharton, 1920

Manhattan Transfer
John Dos Passos, 1925

The Great Gatsby
Francis Scott Fitzgerald,
1925

Tropic of Capricorn
Henry Miller, 1938

The Catcher in the Rye
J. D. Salinger, 1951

Invisible Man
Ralph Ellison, 1952

The Five Cornered Square
Chester Himes, 1957

Breakfast at Tiffany's
Truman Capote, 1958

The Subterraneans
Jack Kerouac, 1958

Last Exit to Brooklyn
Hubert Selby Jr., 1964

Herzog
Saul Bellow, 1964

The Education of
Patrick Silver
Jérôme Charyn, 1976

Nécropolis
Herbert Lieberman, 1976

City of the Dead
James Baldwin, 1979

Bright Lights, Big City
Jay McInerney, 1984

The New York Trilogy
Paul Auster, 1987

The Bonfire of the Vanities
Tom Wolfe, 1987

American Psycho
Bret Easton Ellis, 1991

Jazz
Toni Morrison, 1992

The Alienist
Caleb Carr, 1994

This Side of Brightness
Colum McCann, 1998

Payback
Thomas Kelly, 1998

The Job
Douglas Kennedy, 1999

Cosmopolis
Don DeLillo, 2003

What I Loved
Siri Hustvedt, 2003

Extremely Loud & Incredibly Close
Jonathan Safran Foer, 2005

The Finder
Colin Harrison, 2009

Open City
Teju Cole, 2012

City on Fire
Garth Risk Hallberg, 2016

30 pop figures born in New York

Benny Carter
Jazzman (1907–2003)

Burt Lancaster
Actor, director (1913–1994)

Diane Arbus
Photographer (1923–1971)

Maria Callas
Singer, soprano (1923–1977)

Joseph Heller
Author (1923–1999)

Lauren Bacall
Actress (1924–2014)

Sammy Davis Jr
Dancer, singer,
actor (1925–1990)

Harry Belafonte
Singer, actor,
producer (1927)

Stanley Kubrick
Director, screenwriter,
producer, photographer
(1928–1999)

Hubert Selby Jr
Author (1928–2004)

John Cassavetes
Actor, screenwriter,
director (1929–1989)

Woody Allen
Actor, screenwriter,
director (1935)

Don DeLillo
Author (1936)

Jane Fonda
Actress, producer (1937)

Al Pacino
Actor, producer (1940)

Arthur Garfunkel
Singer (1941)

Martin Scorsese
Director, producer (1942)

Barbara Streisand
Actress, singer, director,
producer (1942)

Sylvester Stallone
Actor, director,
screenwriter,
producer (1946)

Whoopi Goldberg
Actress, comedian,
producer (1955)

Eddie Murphy
Actor, singer, comedian,
producer (1961)

Michael Jordan
Basketball player,
actor (1963)

Lenny Kravitz
Singer, musician (1964)

Ben Stiller
Actor, comedian, director,
screenwriter, producer
(1965)

Mike Tyson
Boxer (1966)

Jay-Z
Rapper, producer (1969)

Sophia Coppola
Director, actress, producer,
screenwriter (1971)

Tupac Shakur
Rapper, actor (1971–1996)

Scarlett Johansson
Actress, singer (1984)

Lady Gaga
Singer, producer (1986)

50 cult songs about New York

'14th Street'
Rufus Wainwright, 2003

'110th Street & Fifth Avenue'
Tito Puente, 2008

'44th Street Suite'
McCoy Tyner, 1991

'51st Street Blues'
Charles Mingus, 1957

'53rd & 3rd'
The Ramones, 1976

'A Letter to the
New York Post'
Public Enemy, 1991

'Across 110th Street'
Bobby Womack, 1972

'All the Critics Love U
in New York City'
Prince, 1982

'An Open Letter to NYC'
Beastie Boys, 2004

'Autumn in New York'
Frank Sinatra, 1949

'Avenue B'
Iggy Pop, 1999

'Avenue of the Americas
(51st Street)'
Moondog, 1953

'A Heart in New York'
Simon & Garfunkel, 1982

'The Blues
(Lenox Avenue Suite)'
Artie Shaw, 1940

'Broadway Blues'
Ornette Coleman, 1968

'Central Park West'
John Coltrane, 1960

'Chelsea Girls'
Nico, 1967

'Chelsea Hotel N°2'
Leonarwd Cohen, 1974

'Chelsea Morning'
Joni Mitchell, 1969

'C.R.E.A.M.'
Wu Tang Clan, 1993

**'Down and Out in
New York City'**
James Brown, 1973

'Empire State of Mind'
Jay-Z featuring Alicia Keys,
2009

'Gotham'
Animal Collective, 2012

**'Greenwich Village Folk
Song Salesman'**
Nancy Sinatra & Lee
Hazlewood, 1967

**'Hard Times in
New York Town'**
Bob Dylan, 1962

'I'll Take New York'
Tom Waits, 1987

'I'm Waiting for the Man'
The Velvet Underground,
1967

'Incident on 57ᵗʰ Street'
Bruce Springsteen, 1973

'Living for the City'
Stevie Wonder, 1973

'Manhattan Skyline'
MFSB, 1980

'Midsummer New York'
Yoko Ono / Plastic Ono
Band, 1970

'New York'
Cat Power, 2008

'New York (Ya Out There)'
Rakim, 1997

'New York City Blues'
Duke Ellington, 1947

'New York City Cops'
The Strokes, 2001

**'New York I Love You (But
You're Bringing Me Down)'**
LCD Soundsystem, 2007

'New York Is Killing Me'
Gil Scott-Heron, 2010

'New York, New York'
Liza Minelli, 1977

'New York, New York'
Grandmaster Flash
& The Furious Five, 1983

'New York State of Mind'
Billy Joel, 1976

'NY State of Mind'
Nas, 1994

'Off Broadway'
George Benson, 1980

'Subway Train'
New York Dolls, 1973

'Spring in Manhattan'
Tony Bennett, 1963

'Streets of New York'
Kool G Rap, 1990

**'Take the Country
to NY City'**
Bohannon, 1981

'The Apple Stretching'
Grace Jones, 1982

'Times Square'
Marianne Faithfull, 1983

**'What New York
Used to Be'**
The Kills, 2008

'Yeah! New York'
Yeah Yeah Yeahs, 2003

50 cult films about New York (1950–2010)

All About Eve
Joseph L. Mankiewicz, 1950

Rear Window
Alfred Hitchcock, 1954

On the Waterfront
Elia Kazan, 1954

Shadows
John Cassavetes, 1959

Breakfast at Tiffany's
Blake Edwards, 1961

West Side Story
Jerome Robbins
and Robert Wise, 1961

Chelsea Girls
Andy Warhol, 1963

Flaming Creatures
Jack Smith, 1963

Mean Streets
Martin Scorsese, 1963

Rosemary's Baby
Roman Polanski, 1968

Macadam Cowboy
John Schlesinger, 1969

French Connection
William Friedkin, 1971

Klute
Alan J. Pakula, 1971

Shaft
Gordon Park, 1971

The Godfather
Francis Ford Coppola, 1972

Serpico
Sydney Lumet, 1973

Dog Day Afternoon
Sydney Lumet, 1975

Taxi Driver
Martin Scorsese, 1976

Annie Hall
Woody Allen, 1977

Saturday Night Fever
John Badham, 1977

New York, New York
Martin Scorsese, 1977

Manhattan
Woody Allen, 1979

The Warriers
Walter Hill, 1979

Fame
Alan Parker, 1980

Maniac
William Lustig, 1980

New York 1997
John Carpenter, 1981

Downtown 81
Edo Bertoglio, 1981

Wild Style
Charlie Ahearn, 1983

**Once Upon a Time
in America**
Sergio Leone, 1984

After Hours
Martin Scorsese, 1985

Year of the Dragon
Michael Cimino, 1985

**Desperately Seeking
Susan**
Susan Seidelman, 1985

When Harry Met Sally…
Rob Reiner, 1989

The King of New York
Abel Ferrara, 1990

Alice
Woody Allen, 1990

Bad Lieutenant
Abel Ferrara, 1992

Carlito's Way
Brian de Palma, 1993

Clockers
Spike Lee, 1995

Smoke
Wayne Wang, 1995

Men in Black
Barry Sonnenfeld, 1997

Donnie Brasco
Mike Newell, 1997

Eyes Wide Shut
Stanley Kubrick, 1999

American Psycho
Mary Harron, 2000

Spider-Man
Sam Raimi, 2002

Gangs of New York
Martin Scorsese, 2002

25ᵗʰ Hour
Spike Lee, 2002

We Own the Night
James Gray, 2007

I Am Legend
Francis Lawrence, 2007

The Visitor
Thomas McCarthy, 2008

Black Swan
Darren Aronofsky, 2010

Overheard about New York

'Can we actually "know" the universe? My God, it's hard enough finding your way around in Chinatown.'

Woody Allen

'New York is a city where you could be frozen to death in the midst of a busy street and nobody would notice.'

Bob Dylan

'Whoever is born in New York is ill-equipped to deal with any other city: all other cities seem, at best, a mistake, and, at worst, a fraud. No other city is so spitefully incoherent.'

James Baldwin

'In New York you've got to have all the luck.'

Charles Bukowski

« Il y a quelque chose dans l'air de New York qui rend le sommeil inutile. »

Simone de Beauvoir

'New York is a different country. Maybe it ought to have a separate government. Everybody thinks differently, they just don't know what the hell the rest of the United States is.'

Henry Ford

'When it's three o'clock in New York, it's still 1938 in London.'

Bette Midler

'Fourteen years in New York is like twenty-seven years anywhere else in the world.'

Jay McInerney

'It is ridiculous to set a detective story in New York City. New York City is itself a detective story.'

Agatha Christie

'A hundred times have I thought New York is a catastrophe and fifty times: it is a beautiful catastrophe.'

Le Corbusier

Index

Bibliography

New York
New York : Chronique d'une ville sauvage, Jérôme Charyn,
Gallimard, Paris, 1994
Histoire de New York, François Weil, Fayard, Paris, 2005
New York : Histoires, promenades, anthologie et dictionnaire,
edited by Pauline Peretz, Robert Laffont,
Paris, 2009
*Unforgotten New York, Legendary Spaces of the Twentieth-Century
Avant-Garde*, David Brun-Lambert, John Short,
David Tanguy, Prestel, Londres, 2015

Billie Holiday
L'Épopée du jazz, tome 1 : du blues au bop, Franck Bergerot,
Gallimard, Paris, 1991
Lady Sings The Blues, Billie Holiday, Parenthèses Éditions,
Paris, 2003
Billie Holiday, Sylvia Fol, Folio, Paris, 2005
Lady Day : Histoire d'amours, Alain Gerber, Le Livre de Poche,
Paris, 2008
Ascenseur pour le jazz : Une histoire du jazz, Julien Delli Fiori,
Éditions de la Martinière, Paris, 2010
New York City Jazz, Elizabeth Dodd Brinkofski, Arcadia
Publishing, Mt. Pleasant, 2013
With Billie, Julia Blackburn, Jonathan Cape Ltd, London, 2005

Jack Kerouac
La Beat Generation : La révolution hallucinée, Alain Dister,
Gallimard, Paris, 1997
Memory Babe, a Critical Biography of Jack Kerouac,
Gerald Nicosia, Puffin, London, 1986
Angelheaded Hipster: Life of Jack Kerouac, Steve Turner,
Bloomsbury Publishing plc, London, 1996
Jack Kerouac: King of the Beats, Barry Miles, Henry Holt and
Co., New York City, 1998
Beat Generation, une anthologie, Gérard-Georges Lemaire,
Éditions Al Dante, Marseille, 2004

Kerouac et la Beat Generation, Jean-François Duval, PUF, Paris, 2012
Beat generation : New York, San Francisco, Paris, catalogue, Philippe-Alain Michaud, Centre Georges Pompidou, Paris, 2016

Robert De Niro
Robert De Niro Sr. (1922–1993), Bruno Gaudichon, Valère Bertrand, Ivana Salander, Somogy éditions d'Art, Paris, 2005
Taxi Driver, Amy Taubin, British Film Institute, London, 2000
Steve Schapiro: Taxi Driver, Paul Duncan, Taschen, Paris, 2013
Taxi Driver, Richard Elman, Paul Schrader, Bantam Books, New York City, 1976
Robert De Niro: Anatomy of an Actor, Karina Longworth, Glenn Kenny, Phaidon Press, New York City, 2014
De Niro: A Life, Shawn Levy, Crown Archetype, New York City, 2014

Andy Warhol
The Andy Warhol Diaries, edited by Pat Hackett, Simon & Schuster, New York City, 1989
I'll Be Your Mirror: The Selected Andy Warhol Interviews, edited by Kenneth Goldsmith, Da Capo Press, Boston, 2004
The Philosophy of Andy Warhol (From A to B and Back Again), Andy Warhol, Harcourt Brace Jovanovich, San Diego, 1975
Warhol Spirit, Cécile Guilbert, Grasset & Fasquelle, Paris, 2008
Andy Warhol, biographie, Mériam Korichi, Folio, Paris, 2009
Andy Warhol n'est pas un grand artiste, Hector Obalk, Flammarion, Paris, 2015

Authors

David Brun-Lambert

is an authority on pop culture and modern cultural avant-gardes. He is a journalist, radio producer, screenwriter and the author of several books, including *Electrochoc* with Laurent Garnier (Flammarion, 2003), *Nina Simone, une vie* (Flammarion, 2005) and *Unforgotten New York* with John Short and David Tanguy (Prestel, 2015).

MAAAD.fr

Founded by the artistic director duo Michael Prigent and Aurélie Pollet at the start of The Parisianer project, the creative agency MAAAD showcases illustration and artists through constantly changing productions based on a collaborative and inventive approach.

Aurélie Pollet

Illustrator, author of graphic novels and documentaries, director and screenwriter of animated films, artistic director Aurélie Pollet brings together a whole host of different forms of artistic expression.

David Tanguy

is the founder and director of the London design studio Praline. He has collaborated with the V&A, The Barbican and the publisher Taschen, he directed the graphic design of the exhibition *Designing 007: 50 years of Bond Style* and is the author of the book *Unforgotten New York* with David Brun-Lambert and John Short (Prestel, 2015).

'This island, floating in river water
like a diamond iceberg, call it
New York, name it whatever you like;
the name hardly matters because,
[…] one is only in search of a city,
a place to hide, to lose or
discover oneself.'

Truman Capote, *The Dogs Bark*, 1973

Texts: David Brun-Lambert
Illustrations: Aurélie Pollet
Artistic direction, illustrations: MAAAD
Art director and design: David Tanguy, Praline

Our profound thanks go to Fabienne Kriegel,
Laurence Lehoux, Jérôme Layrolles, Anne Schuliar and
to Éditions du Chêne – E/P/A.

General director: Fabienne Kriegel
Editorial Manager: Laurence Lehoux
Editorial Assistant: Sandrine Rosenberg
Art director: Sabine Houplain, assisted by Claire Panel
Production: Marion Lance
Photogravure: APS Chromostyle

Translation © Edition du Chêne – Hachette Livre, 2018
English translation and proofreading by
Rebecca Stoakes and Laura Gladwin for Cillero & de Motta
English layout: Vincent Lanceau

Published by Éditions du Chêne
(58, rue Jean Bleuzen, 92178 Vanves Cedex)
Printed in Spain by Estella Graficas
Copyright registration: April 2018
ISBN: 978-2-81231-781-1
53/5254/6-01